SERVANT
SONS &

DAUGHTERS

ANASTASYA LAVERDIERE

SERVANT SONS & DAUGHTERS
Copyright © 2017 by Anastasya Laverdiere

ISBN: 978-1-4866-1483-7   Printed in Canada

Word Alive Press
131 Cordite Road, Winnipeg, MB R3W 1S1
www.wordalivepress.ca

Library and Archives Canada Cataloguing in Publication

Laverdiere, Anastasya, author
    Servant sons and daughters : serving Father God from a place of sonship / Anastasya Laverdiere.

Issued in print and electronic formats.
ISBN 978-1-4866-1483-7 (softcover).--ISBN 978-1-4866-1484-4 (ebook)

    1. Children of God. 2. Children of God--Biblical teaching. 3. God--Fatherhood. 4. God--Fatherhood--Biblical teaching. 5. God (Christianity)--Fatherhood. 6. God (Christianity)--Fatherhood--Biblical teaching. 7. God--Worship and love. 8. God (Christianity)--Worship and love. 9. God--Worship and love--Biblical teaching. I. Title.

BT153.F3L39 2017   231'.1   C2017-903657-2
                                                      C2017-903658-0

To all my brothers and sisters in this royal family of God,
destined to live lives of fullness in the love of our Father.

CONTENTS

Acknowledgements   vii

Introduction   ix

Author's Note   xiii

PART I: What Matters Most...

1. God Desired a Family   8

2. Verdict Overturned   20

PART II: The Children's Clothing

3. The Robe   43

4. The Ring   47

5. The Sandals   54

6. The Celebration   65

PART III: Devoted Sons

7. A Licence to Sin?   73

8. Free to Serve   84

9. A Labour of Love   94

PART IV: The Ultimate Servant Son

10. Developing Royal Dispositions   103

Conclusion   127

ACKNOWLEDGEMENTS

It certainly takes a team to bring a book together, which is why I would like to thank my husband Joel for your friendship, support, and willingness to come alongside me on this journey. Your insights have brought clarity and fullness to my writing.

I am very grateful for Tom Buller for his work in editing this book, which brought it to a place I could not have reached on my own.

Much thanks as well to Sylvia St.Cyr for guiding me through the publishing process and being there to answer all my questions with such kindness!

To all those who read through this manuscript at different stages of its development, your feedback and kind words gave me the courage and confidence to pursue this publication. You all have been such a blessing to me—thank you!

INTRODUCTION

I was privileged to grow up in a Christian home attending church regularly. My family was always the first to arrive and the last to leave. All of my life, my parents modeled servanthood so well I had a pretty good idea what it meant to live your life in service to God. However, in all the good—the church life, Sunday school, the summer camps, etc.—something was still missing, something crucial.

At fifteen I received Jesus Christ as my Lord and Savior and then set out working to "please Him" in my everyday life. I expressed much thankfulness for His grace and favor accepting me into His kingdom.

The problem was my behavior often arose more from fear than a place of joy. I was so grateful He wasn't going to throw me in Hell—well, at least as long as I wasn't sinning too badly. Although God's grace is not something to take advantage of (an idea we'll explore in this book), living with such a fearful revelation of

> Excellent on the outside, empty within

God kept Him at a distance in my thinking. In my mind He was elusive, harsh, and a bit hard to please. Therefore I worked *for* Him, being excellent on the outside but feeling empty on the inside.

How could this be? I was born again and sincerely desired to walk with God. And yet a gaping hole existed in my heart that I didn't know how to fill. I tried many things: relationships, perfectionism, working harder, reading the Bible more, etc., until eventually giving up. At twenty-two, in the midst of a mess of a life I'd made, I came to the end of myself and there in the fire I found the key I had been looking for. Wrestling with continuous panic attacks, I came to the end of my human strength and God's power led me to one simple verse. *"There is no fear in love, but perfect love casts out fear. For fear has to do with punishment and whoever fears has not been perfected in love"* (I John 4:18). All I knew was fear. Where was this "perfect love" that was supposed to "cast out" my fear? Where did it come from and how could I get it?

I can remember being a teenager and wanting to do what teenagers often want to do—be a bit rebellious. I had my heart set on attending a party with some of my friends. My parents, being good and loving, knew this would not be the best environment for me. On this particular day they did not choose to enact their authority and forbid me to go. My dad, the king of wise one-liners, simply left me with a powerful statement as I excitedly got ready to leave the house. Instead of lecturing me on the dangers and choices I would soon face, he simply said, **"Remember who you are…"**

At that time I was still very much discovering who exactly I was, but I knew what he meant. He was reminding me to remember the Christian values I had been brought up on. In this way, remembering who I was would protect me from involving myself in things contrary to my nature. Knowing who we are and having a solid identity gives us a strong sense of direction in life—not only in the natural but the spiritual sense, too. When I left the house that day, I represented not only myself but my family and my father. A deep sense of purpose and responsibility entered my heart.

Understanding the relationship we can have with God as His children, and His heart towards us as our Father, is the foundation for everything else we do as Christians. Without security in our position with God, we cannot fully live out our callings to their potential. It is a debilitating thing to try living without an inner sense of being loved and accepted, and no less debilitating to try to serve a Holy God from a distance. We can never be comfortable in the presence of someone when we are unsure of their welcome. If our approach to God is still somewhat timid and unsure, our connection to His resources will be intermittent at best. Allowing ourselves to be "perfected" in His love through the washing of His word will set us into a new place of freedom in our walk as Christians. This is how the Christian life becomes an adventure, ever discovering more about who we are and who our Father is. This revelation will be life and freedom for us.

This book explores the great relationship God longs for and calls us to through salvation. It seeks to move from the potentially crippling state of uncertainty in our identity towards the powerfully freeing revelation of true identity as sons and daughters of God.

Paul said it was essential to know *"how wide, how long, how high and how deep"* the love of God is in order to receive the *"fullness of life and power that comes from God"* (Ephesians 3:19, NLT). I echo his prayer that as you read this book you too would divinely discover the "fullness of life and power that comes from God!"

I pray as the Holy Spirit illuminates these words He will:

...grant you to be strengthened with power through his Spirit in your inner being, so that Christ may dwell in your hearts through faith— that you, being rooted and grounded in love, may have strength to comprehend with all the saints what is the breadth and length and height and depth, and to know the love of Christ that surpasses knowledge, that you may be filled with all the fullness of God.

—Ephesians 3:16–19, ESV

Read on and discover all He has for you in the fullness of His word!

AUTHOR'S NOTE

Many scriptures in this book as well as the text itself refer to sons without the addition of daughters. This doesn't mean females are not included. For example, I John 3:I reads, *"How great is the love the Father has bestowed upon us that we should be called the sons of God."* The Greek word for sons is TÉKVOV translated téknon (tek'-non) which means child, daughter, or son. Although the word "son" generally means a direct male descendant, in the Bible it has many uses referring to a characteristic or identity, e.g. "sons of Aaron" were priests and the "sons of Asaph" were musicians (I Chronicles 25:I). As Galatians 3:7 clarifies, it is *"those of faith who are the sons of Abraham"* and since now there is therefore *"neither male nor female"* through salvation (Galatians 3:28–29), women can freely be included in the many verses that reference the sons of God! The use of the term "sons" represents a relationship open to all humankind, which we will be exploring in this book.

PART I

WHAT MATTERS
MOST...

A PICTURE HANGS IN MY ROOM WHERE I DO MOST OF MY WRITING AND Bible study. It's a photo of a kitten staring into a large mirror and its reflection is a fierce lion staring back at him. The caption reads, "What matters most is how you see yourself." Nowhere is this truer than when it comes to the life of a believer.

Judges 6–8 introduces us to a young man in the Bible who is presented with an impossible task after first being addressed by a name he was completely surprised to be associated with. This young man is Gideon, and Gideon had a problem. When the angel of the Lord came to visit him offering a solution to Israel's current state of deprivation and starvation, Gideon had more than a few objections.

The story begins in Judges 6:11 where the angel of the Lord, by whatever divine decision was made in heaven, decides to come down and call Gideon to action.[1] *"When the angel of the Lord appeared*

---

1   Different translations translate" the angel of the Lord" as the Lord Himself. As the conversation continues we see strong evidence that it was indeed the Lord speaking to Gideon, rather than a messenger of sorts for example when He indicates such phrases as "I am with you...did I not send you?" Whether the Lord Himself or a messenger, the message still came from God to Gideon.

to Gideon, he said, 'The Lord is with you, mighty warrior'" (v.12). Gideon responds with a telling rebuttal, revealing his perspective of himself and the people's proximity to God.

"Pardon me, my Lord?" Gideon replied. "But if the Lord is with us, why has all this happened to us?" Gideon makes a subtle, indirect accusation towards God of being absent from the lives of His people. The verses preceding this text, however, clearly indicate that it wasn't a matter of God leaving them—they left Him.

God, in His grace, doesn't feel the need to defend Himself. He had something bigger to do—He had to get Gideon *seeing* properly! Mighty warrior is certainly a powerful title, one which Gideon was in no shape yet to receive.

After God repeats His command and promises to be with Gideon, Gideon is still stuck on one thing: "I can't, because my family is the weakest in Manasseh and I am the least in my family." Gideon's view of himself was, at best, one of inferiority and this type of insecurity is not uncommon to people. More than a few men and women in the Bible had trouble believing what God said about them and it is something many of us face at some point. "Who are you?" is both the life of faith's constant challenge and our enemy the devil's constant taunt.

Gideon missed a few key points in his conversation with the Lord. The biggest point: Gideon's ability to be successful would not depend on his own shortcomings but rather would be rooted in God's promise to be with Him. Gideon had a skewed view of just how much he and all God's people meant to God which was evident by the way he indirectly blamed God for all the bad things that had happened to Israel. He concluded that the absence of God's

4

miracles was a sure sign God had abandoned them. Gideon doubted God and put a serious negative claim on God's character. If God could abandon His people at any point, then there was a limit to His love and, in Gideon's mind, He and all the people had stepped out of it.

This happens to us, does it not? When we aren't sure exactly where we stand with God, we're often a little shaky in our daily walk with Him. If we view Him as absent from our lives in the least bit, we will not turn to Him for the things we need let alone approach Him with any kind of boldness for the things we want.

There doesn't seem to be much recognition in Gideon's response of the sin Israel had committed against God, or else I would be able to discuss here one major barrier to our acceptance of our position to God: shame. But we will be discussing that later in this book. I find it amazing that God did not retort the misinformed claims of this ignorant young man but perhaps, in God's poise, we see a powerful insight into what He really cares about. His first address to this young man says it all. God calls Gideon something he had never been called before and certainly did not perceive in himself—"Mighty Warrior." Why did God start things out this way? It seems the Father's most important concern is to get Gideon to start seeing himself differently. God had to get Gideon to accept a truth about his identity that would eventually enable him to do what God was calling him to do. He deals with Gideon's identity before He ever gives him his first assignment.

Identity is one area which comes under great attack in our world. Society is full of lies telling us we need more of this and that to matter—be it beauty, finances, possessions, popularity, social media following, etc. Things such as these can seek to determine how much we're worth and define who we are. If we live without a good answer in our souls for the constant question, "Who are you?" we cannot stand against the onslaught of attacks we will face in everyday life. This question will come to you and we must find our response within the pages of the word God has given to us.

We do not define ourselves blindly, like picking a name out of a hat hoping it fits. We have a clear definition laid out for us in God's word, a definition already in place that we must pick up and apply to ourselves with tenacity. The Bible is the "word of Truth" (2 Timothy 2:15)—and how we need truth today! If Gideon never believed what God was saying about him, the exploits recorded in chapters 7–8 of Judges would not have been possible. If Moses insisted He was not who God said he was (Exodus 3–4:18) a nation would not have been freed from the grip of the Pharaoh. We have no idea what lies in the destinies God has designed each of us for, and we will never see them realized on the earth without first recognizing that we have been designed. This is a confidence in who we are and who He is, and a determination to use what we've been given to accomplish His work on this earth. No matter what other title you may have in the kingdom of God—preacher, teacher, evangelist, wife, father, etc., you have one you must settle in your heart above them all: Son. Contained within the depths of this revelation are security, freedom, love, authority, power, and true devotion.

We know somewhere along the way Gideon "got it." I love what Zebah and Zalmunna had to say about Gideon, encountering him after his dramatic transformation from a weak nobody to the Mighty Warrior God had said he was.

"Then Gideon asked Zebah and Zalmunna, 'The men you killed at Tabor—what were they like?' 'Like you,' they replied. 'They all **had the look of a king's son.'"**

—Judges 8:18, NLT (emphasis added)

Wow, now he had a *look* about him and it was royalty. As we let the glorious truth of our identity in Christ fill our hearts and transform our lives, we too will have a look about us. We will be identified as a member of the family of God both by our enemies and those who have yet to come into the family. This is going to be one amazing journey! Come and see what lies ahead.

GOD DESIRED A FAMILY

Even before He made the world, God loved us and chose us in Christ to be holy and without fault in His eyes. God decided in advance to adopt us into His own family by bringing us to Himself through Jesus Christ. This is what He wanted to do, and it gave Him great pleasure.
—Ephesians 1:4–6, NLT

THIS...IS WHAT HE *WANTED* TO DO! DID YOU CATCH THAT? AS MY British friends would say, "full stop," we need to grasp something here. Can you get a sense of God's priorities as He laid out the foundation of the world? Genesis 1 and on tells us all about God's magnificent creation of the earth and everything in it—plants, animals, the sky, the oceans, the stars, it's all fascinating—but here in Ephesians 1 we see God had something else in mind even before He created everything else. His desire was not merely to create a beautiful art project filled with wonderful and amazing things. Though He delighted in all He made, it wasn't enough for Him. He desired to make a creature with whom He could have relationship. He made a creature He intended to interact with: mankind made in His image and special compared to all the other created things. Before the foundation of the earth, God desired to bring us into His family.

God instituted the family unit when He spoke to Adam and Eve to be fruitful and multiply (Genesis 1:28) and fill the earth with children. He created marriage between a man and a woman to be an act that would bring them into total unity of "one flesh" (Genesis 2:24). God continued to show how much the family unit mattered to Him when He spoke within the Ten Commandment laws which protected parents and honoured the purity of the husband/wife relationship (Exodus 20:12,14,17). In the New Testament, Jesus continued to take up the cause for the family, teaching on the subject and the sanctity of marriage as He spoke against divorce under certain circumstances (Matthew 19:3–12). Paul and many of the New Testament authors gave commands and advice concerning family matters to the churches they served (Ephesians 6:1–11, Colossians 3:20–21).

God loves family! After all, He designed it. Throughout the Old Testament we see many statements of God's desire to be known by His people as a Father. Deuteronomy 1:31 beautifully describes the Lord's fatherly relationship to His people: *"there in the wilderness. . . there you saw how the Lord your God carried you as a Father carries His son. . ."* Again, in Psalm 103:13: *"as a Father has compassion on His children, so the Lord has compassion on all those who fear Him."* In Jeremiah 3:19, God displays His broken heart over His people's unfaithfulness: *"I would love to treat you as my own children"* He laments, *"I wanted nothing more than to give you this beautiful land. . .I looked forward to your calling me 'Father' and I wanted you never to turn from me."*

Can you hear His heart here? He wanted nothing more than to be called Israel's Father. Here the title He was requesting was not Lord, not Master, but Father. Fatherhood is a position God desires to hold in the life of His people; "I am Israel's Father..." (Jeremiah 31:9). Many men shirk the responsibility of fatherhood when they realize all it will demand of them. It will require everything of them. A father protects, a father guides, a father loves and builds up His children. A father disciplines for the good of His child. A father sacrifices his own wants and desires for the good of his family. A father is a leader, and leadership will demand him to mature. But even the best earthly Father cannot compare to the greatness of our Heavenly One. He is a Father to the fatherless, His love and compassion are endless, and He is completely righteous and good.

In Jesus' instruction to us concerning prayer, He lays out the preferred title to address the supreme God. *"Our Father who art in heaven..."* (Matthew 6:9, emphasis added). In this prayer model is the fulfillment of the words given to Israel repeated to the church of the New Testament, "I looked forward to your calling me 'Father.'" Through the words of Jesus, Father God encourages His children, "I want you to come to me and when you do please address me as your Father. It is from this place that I will answer you and treat you as dearly loved children of mine."

We must come to Him addressing Him as He is. We must receive Him the way He has requested we receive Him—as our Father. In the beginning—before the beginning—God desired a family to Father. In the pages ahead, we will further illustrate that we are the realization of that desire. May the revelation that God *wanted* you and *created you to be with you* sink into your heart. This was always his plan, to be your Father and to have you as His child. His church is a family in which you belong! Let your heart exclaim truly, "I was always wanted. Now I am His and He is mine...forever!"

THE SPIRIT OF ADOPTION

But when the proper time had fully come, God sent His son, born of a woman, born subject to the (regulations of) the Law, To purchase the freedom of. . .those who were subject to the Law, that we might be adopted and have sonship conferred upon us (and be recognized as God's sons).

—Galatians 4:4–5, AMP

If we simply let scripture speak, it will do a very good job laying out for us the idea that we are children of God. In more than a few places in the word, scripture states that we become a part of the family of God upon acceptance of Christ's finished work on the cross—a work He was *sent* to do by a loving Father who desperately wanted to get his creation back!

We're probably not struggling with the fact that scripture says we are God's children. The part we struggle with is the deeper revelation of what this truth really means to us which penetrates our hearts and, as a result, transforms our lives.

I have known only a few friends who were adopted as children. In speaking with my friends, they revealed a great sense of thankfulness, and although there may have been some curiosity as to who their birth parents were or what situation led to adoption, overall these adoptees had found their identity and security in the family they now belonged to and were very happy in doing so.

By looking at the process of adoption, we can get an even clearer sense of what Paul is saying here and what the concept of adoption means to us. In many countries, adoption requires a complete transfer of something called filiation. Filiation is the recognized legal status of relationships between family members, specifically parent-child relationships.[2] During the transfer of filiation, the adoptee becomes completely unaffiliated with their former parenting figure, either biological or not, and is now completely affiliated with a new parent and a new family.

Scripture highlights a similar process that takes place for the new believer at the point of salvation. In 2 Corinthians 5:17, we learn that *"anyone who belongs to Christ has become a new person. The old life is gone; a new life has begun!"* Whoever we were before changes when we accept Christ as our Savior, as well as whom we were affiliated with. Colossians 1:13 tells us that when we received God the Father's offer of salvation through His Son, He *"delivered us from the power (or kingdom in other translations) of darkness and hath translated us into the kingdom of the kingdom of His beloved Son"* (WBT). We actually changed our residency in this whole exchange. The word "translated" found in this scripture means to bear, carry or move from one place, position, etc., to another or to transfer. We have literally been transferred from the present kingdom of the earth into the Kingdom of heaven and that kingdom operates as the precious and very real family of God. The definition of the word "translate" provides an even greater depth to our understanding to what has happened through salvation. It clarifies that to "translate" is "to change from one place, state, form

---

2   "Filiation",   Law   Dictionary.   http://www.lawyerintl.com/law-dictionary/2994-filiation. (accessed August 9, 2017)

or appearance to another: transform"[3]. The "translation" process at salvation when we're adopted into the family of God has the power to actually change our nature as we let the culture of our new Kingdom family develop us into the people we really are: *"citizens of heaven, where the Lord Jesus Christ lives"* (Philippians 3:20).

Adoption is a permanent and legal process both on earth and in the supernatural. It is complete. Old ties are severed and new ones are established. Adoptees are issued a new birth certificate, further signifying the brand new affiliation with a different family. In salvation, we too are issued a new spiritual birth certificate indicating the date and time of our new birth and labeling us children of God. John 1:12–13 gives assurance of this new birth: *"but to all who believed Him and accepted Him, He gave the right to become children of God. They are reborn—not with a physical birth resulting from human passion or plan, but a birth that comes from God"* (NLT).

We are born of God, anew, fresh and prepped to get back in line with all He planned for us to be. He assumes full responsibility as our Father indicated in the promises He gave to care for us (Matthew 6), to lead us (Psalm 32:8), protect us (Psalm 121:7), provide for us (Malachi 3) and so much more. We now must see our new form. We have to let our hearts receive this new birth and recognize we have changed affiliation so we begin to act like it. Everything we do as Christians will come out of how we truly see ourselves deep inside. If we see ourselves as children of heaven, we will live

---

3   "Translate." Merriam-Webster.com. 2017. https://merriam-webster.com (accessed May 1, 2017)

appropriately, not getting caught up in what's temporal but living for what is eternal. If we see ourselves as children of heaven, we will seek to connect with our "true home" often through prayer and worship, seeking out the presence of our Father and the communion with Holy Spirit and the Son. If we are children of God, we will love our family and commit ourselves to the work God invites us to do with Him during our time on earth.

> Everything we do as Christians will come out of how we truly see ourselves deep inside.

Romans 8:15–17 reiterates almost word for word what Galatians 4:4–5 tells us, except it spends a bit more time on a new idea—our inheritance: *"and if we are His children then we are (His) heirs also, heirs of God and fellow heirs with Christ (sharing His inheritance with Him)"*(AMP). As sons and daughters we are heirs of God. An heir is someone who inherits or has a right of inheritance in the property of another. And what is this inheritance? Well, we're about to take a very in-depth look into our inheritance as children of God, but first we must receive the revelation that we truly are sons and daughters. Let His Spirit of adoption, the Holy Spirit, cry out from within you, "Abba, Father," knowing full well you have received the authority to do so having become His child.

As His Spirit bears witness to this truth within our hearts, we will let the reality of it transform us into the appearance of sons and daughters of God. Then, we can truly exclaim also with a glad revelation, *"Behold what manner of love the Father has bestowed upon us that we should be called the Sons of God!"* (1 John 3:3)

REFLECTION QUESTIONS

1) How true does it feel to you that God is your Father and has desired you as His child?
2) What are some ways your belief about this affects you in your everyday life?
3) From the many verses covered in this section about your new "affiliation" as a child of God, which ones stand out most to you? Is there any part of this revelation you still struggle to believe and personalize?

I encourage you to mediate on these verses and ask the Father to reveal to you the truth of them concerning you.

JUST CALL ME DADDY

So you have not received a spirit that makes you fearful slaves Instead, you received God's Spirit when He adopted you as His own children. Now we call Him, "Abba, Father." For His Spirit joins with our spirit to affirm that we are God's children.

—Romans 8:15–16, NLT

I hope by now the revelation that you are indeed a child of God is penetrating your heart. This revelation, once received, redefines how we address the God of the universe. Before our adoption took place and was finalized through faith and acceptance of what Christ has done, we may have been timid and not sure what to call Him. Now, through His own design, we are to approach Him using a much closer term. We are able to address Him as Father. "Abba Father" is an affectionate, endearing term used within the context of a close and connected relationship. But the term "Abba" used here in Romans 8 adds an even more challenging depth of revelation to what may be our typical understanding of Father. Some of us may have experienced broken relationships with our own earthly fathers, which makes it difficult to understand the term. Or perhaps we've learned from well-meaning preachers who advised and endorsed keeping a safe distance in our relationship with God. After all, a perfect and Holy God couldn't actually want us to come *that* close to Him, could He? Although there is debate concerning the translation "daddy" for Abba, and in some cases I agree this translation has been taken too far, I think we would be missing the point Paul is trying to make here in this passage by only discussing the word itself. From Romans 8:15, Paul makes a new distinction for the believers who have accepted Christ, emphasizing they were not to approach God as fearful slaves. Instead they were to come to Him as children. The Vines Expository Dictionary of New Testament Words explains (emphasis added):

> ABBA: is an Aramaic word, found in Mark 14:36; Romans 8:15 and Galatians 4:6. In the Gemara (a Rabbinical commentary on the Mishna, the traditional teaching of the Jews) it is stated that **slaves were forbidden to address the head of the family by this title…** "Abba" is the word framed by the lips of infants, and betokens unreasoning trust.

It approximates to **a personal name** in contrast to "Father," with which it is always joined in the NT. This is probably due to the fact that, abba having practically become a proper name, Greek-speaking Jews added the Greek word pater, "father," from the language they used. "Abba" is the word framed by the lips of infants, and **betokens unreasoning trust; "father" expresses an intelligent apprehension of the relationship. The two together express the love and intelligent confidence of the child.** [4]

This word "Abba" carries the instruction to seek out an "affectionate, dependent relationship"[5] with our Father in which we recognize His power and majesty but also His desire to come close. To feel comfortable using this term, we must internalize the fact that we have truly have joined His family. There is a progression illustrated in the Bible from mankind's closeness with God in the garden, separation at the fall (Genesis 3), and then the pursuit of the Father to restore us back to Himself—the whole thing brought to a climax at the coming of Christ as Messiah. I like this observation, stating, "Biblical history is, among other things, the story of almighty, infinite, eternal, holy, transcendent God initiating and

---

4   Vines, W.E., W.Graham Scroggie, F.F. Bruce, 1966. *Vines Expository Dictionary of New Testament Words*. Fleming H.Revell Company, Old Tappan; New Jersey (pg.9)

5   Helps Word-studies says, "5 Abba (line above)—"Father," also used as the term of tender endearment by a beloved child- i.e. in an affectionate, dependent relationship with their father; "daddy," "papa." (HELPS TM WORD-studies copyright 1987, 2011 By Helps Ministries, Inc.)

developing an increasingly intimate relationship with His people".[6] The change in His preferred titles coincides with the enactment of the new Covenant through Christ. Although even in the Old Testament God reveals His desire to be approached as a tender, loving Father (Jeremiah 3:19), the term Abba offered here in the New Testament writings calls for an even deeper recognition of our proximity to Him as sons and daughters.

God doesn't desire all the formality we may think He does. Consider how odd or annoying it would be if someone insisted on calling you "Mr." or "Mrs." when you've repeatedly asked them to call you by your first name. How distant would it feel if someone you regarded as a close friend always used your formal title in conversation? There is certainly a place and time to use terms depicting the other positions and titles God holds in our life. We call Him Lord as an act of submission and we call Him the Most High as an act of worship, etc. What I'm looking at here is if there is an inability to call Him "Daddy" or "Father" with complete recognition of all the intimacy that term implies, then we may be keeping ourselves at greater distance from God than we recognize. If it would feel too close or even wrong to refer to Him this way, something is blocking you from receiving all He has for you. Everything God has for us is connected to who He is. *"I am the Lord who heals you..."* (Exodus 15:26), "healer" is who He is, therefore healing is what He does. Love, joy, peace, prosperity, and righteousness are not just things He

---

6   From Elohim to Abba; the intimate names of God, student.soul.intervarsity. com (accessed May 1, 2017)

has, they are who He is. Therefore, our connection to these aspects of God must come through our connection with Him.

If addressing God with such intimate terms would feel to you like lessening His honor, or bringing Him down from His position, remember this: He already came down on His own admission once, as the man Jesus. God did not fear losing His position when He came in search of a family. He remained God and

> Everything God has for us is connected to who He is.

there was and is no one and nothing above Him. He will always be the all-powerful, supreme ruler and creator of everything. His kingdom stands forever and the gates of hell will not ever prevail against His church. How humble for the most powerful being to seek out the weakest—but He did. Now He desires that you and I approach Him as children, crying out, "Abba (Daddy) Father," and basking in His love. Giving Him this place *is* honoring Him in one of the greatest ways we can! You call Him Lord, for He is your Lord indeed, now call Him Father for He is that also!

With all the honor and love in your heart, officially announce Him as your Father today, of whom you are so proud and to whom you are so thankful.

VERDICT OVERTURNED

BEFORE WE MOVE ON, ALLOW ME TO EXPOUND THE INCREDIBLE STORY of redemption and what it entails for us who have now experienced the restoration as sons. God had to move past a lot of stuff in order to initiate and proceed with the process of adopting our lost souls back into His family. I mean seriously, what parent considering adoption would look at the offences most of us had stacked against us and still decide to go through with it anyway? Only One with immeasurable grace. In order to restore a broken father/child relationship like this one, God had to move from just mere acquittal to total forgiveness. "Forgiven" is not a verdict the courts typically render, but in the courtroom of Heaven it is the verdict rendered through salvation.

In this courtroom, the most unusual scene takes place. Seated at a table facing the Judge is a man guilty of every accusation brought against him. As the list of offences and lawlessness is read before the court, he hangs his head knowing there is no way he can be acquitted. There is no denying it—he is guilty. He sits in a Holy place where only justice and truth abide, yet within him resides all the filthiness of the earth and its fallen nature. After all accusations are read he is asked to stand to await his sentence—surely an eternity in hell. He has only one person standing with him now, the One with scars in the palms of his hands and feet, One who died a merciless death on a cross many years before the accused even committed any of his crimes. He had met this One only a few years earlier, before he was absent from the body and present with the Lord. In a moment of total remorse, the accused believed the testimony about this man from Galilee and put faith in the word that if he openly declared that this man, Jesus, was Lord and believed in His heart God had raised Him from the dead, he would be saved. And so he did just that.

Now here he is, glad to have but one advocate. "You're all I have!" he exclaims.

The One arrayed in shining garments replies, "I'm all you'll need!"

The Judge assumes His place, the verdict ready to be announced. With every right in the world to pronounce this one guilty and be done with him, He delivers an astounding bombshell, "I see no sin in you, only the righteousness of my Son. I pronounce you not guilty."

Speechlessness and overwhelming relief covers the erring one's face. He knows he has just been let go and with immense gratefulness he goes over to the Son. The pardoned leaps to embrace this Son who so willingly stepped in to take his punishment and overturn the Judge's decision. The forgiven pledges allegiance to the Son forever.

After embracing him back, the Son smiles, turns, and points towards the Judge. "It was all His idea."

With all the bustle in the courtroom, the man had not noticed the Judge was even still there. To his amazement, the Judge gets up from His throne, steps down off His platform, and walks over to him. With wonder and bewilderment in his eyes the plaintiff falls to his knees in worship to thank this Judge for His unexplainable benevolence. Even more incredibly, the Judge stoops down again, places a hand on the humbled beneficiary and says, "Come child, I've been waiting for you to come home." There is an absence of judgement, for all who receive Christ become completely righteous in the eyes of the Father. *"For God made Christ, who never sinned, to be the offering for our sin, so that we could be made right with God through Christ"* (2 Corinthians 5:21).

It was God's pursuit of us that made salvation possible. In all our honor of the Son, which

> It was God's pursuit of us that made salvation possible.

is proper and can never stop, we must not forget that God our Father was the mastermind in the Trinity behind the whole thing. We must see and fall in love with Him.

To receive all God has for us, we must fully accept His Spirit of adoption and believe in His continual desire to actually be close to us. Stretching back to the garden, God made man with the intention to be with mankind. His pursuit has not changed and His desire remains the same.

I have loved You, my people, with an everlasting love. With unfailing love I have drawn you to Myself.

—Jeremiah 31:3

Oh the wonder of it all! What a glorious plan and what a magnificent outcome! Receive this truth into your hearts today. You are the object of His affection and He has gone to great lengths to prove it to you!

WHAT YOU DON'T KNOW CAN HURT YOU

In Luke 15:11–32, we find a parable which powerfully illustrates the Father's heart in salvation. It's commonly known as The Parable of the Prodigal (or Lost) Son. Jesus had been trying to teach a bunch of leaders stuck in religion known as the Pharisees a thing or two about the kingdom and the grace of Father God. The Pharisees were quite jaded by Jesus' acceptance of and interaction with sinners, as he had even been so bold as to *"eat with them"* (v. 2). He preceded His final parable on the Lost Son with two less-extensive parables highlighting the Father's heart for any individual who strays from him by comparing them to the worth and value of a precious lost coin or sheep. In this concluding parable, Jesus reveals truths about the heart of the Father that we simply cannot afford to miss.

The story starts by depicting the life of a father and his unruly younger son. The son, apparently convinced he was ready for life on his own, comes to his father and demands his share of the inheritance so he can go his own way. The father agrees and divides up the inheritance for his son, and the young man leaves to do what he has determined to do in his heart. He lives "the life" which seems to serve him well for a while until his father's money runs out and he finds himself helpless and alone in a foreign country. One can only imagine what kind of things he entangled himself with. The older brother points out a few things under the heading of *"wild living"* and entertaining *"prostitutes"* (v. 30). This young son squandered everything his father had given him and paid no attention to the righteous ways of his family. Eventually, the consequences of his life choices started catching up with him. A severe famine came over all the land and the son, having spent all his provision, found himself in need. He then had a revelation which led him on a journey back to his father.

> *When he came to his senses, he said, "How many of my father's hired servants have food to spare and here I am starving to death! I will set out and go back to my father and say to him: Father, I have sinned against heaven and against you.* **I am no longer worthy to be called your son***; make me like one of your hired men." So he got up and went to his father.*
>
> —Luke 15:17–20, NIV (emphasis added)

Here is repentance at its finest! The son came to the end of himself and his resources and recognized his need to return to his father, the fulfiller of all need. I love the fact that scripture says he "came to his senses" because this couldn't be more accurate about what happens when we recognize the insanity of our sin and choose life, receiving the sacrifice of Christ as payment for our sins.

The son prepares his repentance and intends to finish it with this statement, *"I am no longer worthy to be called your son; make me like one of your servants."* If we keep reading in this chapter we will see an out-of-this-world response from a Father who clearly has heavenly priorities in place and because of this, the son never even gets to finish his planned confession.

But while he (the son) was still a long way off, his father saw him and was filled with compassion for him; he **ran** *to his son, threw his arms around him and kissed him. The son said to him, "Father, I have sinned against heaven and against you. I am no longer worthy to be called your son."*

But the Father said to his servants, "Quick! Bring the best robe and put it on him. Put a ring on his finger and sandals on his feet. Bring the fattened calf and kill it. Let's have a feast and celebrate. For **this son of mine** *was dead and is alive again; he was lost and is found."*

—Luke 15:20–24, NIV (emphasis added)

Amazing response isn't it? Not one mention of how the son may have hurt him, even though he would have had every right to stand there with arms crossed and demand his child beg for forgiveness. The father stops his son at a crucial point in the confession: "I am no longer worthy to be called your son..." At first the father appears oblivious to the statement but with a closer look I think we'll find he actually was responding with a series of actions signifying he had no intention of stripping this young man of his position as his son. In fact, when he gives the reason for the celebration he is about to throw, he states, *"this* **son of mine** *was dead and is alive again,"* reinforcing that no demotion had or ever would take place.

This is a moment to pause and let the reality of this scene intrigue our hearts. Despite what the son had done, no matter how far he had gone and how recklessly he managed his father's provision, he was now receiving the most extravagant welcome back not only into his father's house but complete assurance of his eternal welcome in his father's heart.

We're going to take a look into three very important aspects of salvation displayed in the father's reaction. Three lessons our hearts need to learn to live in the fullness of what has been offered through salvation.

JUSTIFICATION

Although you may have heard the concept of justification before, what I've discovered in my own life and sometimes the lives of others is that though we may have head knowledge of the idea of justification, we can be living without heart knowledge or personal knowledge of it for ourselves. And this can negatively affect the way we walk out salvation.

I once heard a Bible teacher define justification this way; justification means "just-as-if-I'd-never sinned." What an extremely accurate thought when weighed against the light that scripture sheds on the subject. There are many verses in the Bible concerning justification through faith alone in Christ!

> *For what does the Scripture say? Abraham believed God and it was counted to him as righteousness. Now to the one who works, his wages are not counted as a gift but as his due. And to the one who does not work but believes in Him who **justifies the ungodly**, his faith is counted as righteousness.*
>
> —Romans 4:3–5, ESV (emphasis added)

This verse brings up an approach that many take towards justification. It's echoed in the response of the son to his father in Luke 15:19: *"Just make me like one of your hired servants"* or in other words, "give me some work to do so that I can feel like I'm earning my way back to You."

Much of the teachings of Paul and the New Testament are geared towards helping the new followers of Christ to recognize that their salvation was no longer tied to their work in keeping the law. A new covenant had been enacted through the death and resurrection of Christ and now this covenant was based on faith. This was a sizeable shift for many hearing Paul's teachings on the subject, including this one found in Ephesians 2:8–9:

> *For it is by grace you have been saved, through faith—and this not from yourselves, it is a gift of God—***not by works*** lest any man should boast.* (NIV, emphasis added)

We find this lesson again in Galatians 2:16:

> *For we know that a person* **is not justified** *by works of the law but through faith in Jesus Christ, so we also have* **believed** *in Jesus Christ, in order to be* **justified** *by faith in Christ and not by works of the law, because by works of the law no one will be* **justified.** (NIV, emphasis added)

Paul is making it clear to his listeners that you cannot be justified by anything you do and justification is given on the basis of faith alone in Christ. These scriptures alone are powerful and the definition of justification itself takes this revelation even further. Justified means to "declare innocent or guiltless."[7] Did you catch that? Declare innocent or guiltless...

If I asked you today if you feel innocent or guiltless before God, what would you say? It helps to move away from a word we may have heard since childhood Sunday school classes, a word we may have grown accustomed to without truly understanding its full meaning.

Let's read Galatians 2:16 again, inserting the full meaning of the word justified. "...so we also have believed in Jesus Christ, in order to be [declared innocent and guiltless] by faith in Christ and not by works of the law."

Back in Luke 15, we see the son was still trying to retain some form of dignity by offering to simply *work* for his father. But the father would have none of it. In fact his sin is never even mentioned by the father. The staggering homecoming his father throws for him makes it seem just as if this son had never sinned.

> *For His unfailing love toward those who fear Him is as great as the height of the heavens above the earth. He has* **removed our sins as far from us as the east is from the west.**
> —Psalm 103:11–12, NLT (emphasis added)

---

7   Justified" dictionary.com. http://www.dictionary.com/browse/justified?s=t (accessed May 2, 2017)

And I will forgive their wickedness, and I will **never again remember their sins**.

—Hebrews 8:12, NLT (emphasis added)

But if we confess our sins to Him, He is faithful and just to forgive us our sins and **cleanse us from all wickedness**.

—1 John 1:9, NLT (emphasis added)

After we repent, God thinks of our sin no more. That's truly incredible. He forgets our sins and no longer counts them against us. Faced with this truth, we have only to ask ourselves the question, do I believe that? Do I *know* my sins are not just forgiven by God but actually forgotten by Him also?

If the son in Luke 15 insisted on paying for his sins and earning his way back to his position with his father, he would have been mirroring what many Christians are stuck in today: trying to earn, whether consciously or subconsciously, the fullness of salvation through some form of work. This is working from a guilty conscience rather than a heart set free by grace. The son had no choice but to move on with the Father in the freedom He was providing.

David, a beautiful representation of someone who embraced concepts of Sonship way before the New Covenant was ever enacted, captures the heart of justification so exquisitely when he writes, *"Blessed are those* **whose lawless deeds are forgiven**, *and* **whose sins are covered**; *blessed is the man* **against whom the Lord will not count his sin**" (Romans 4:7, ESV, emphasis added).

If you have received Christ as your Lord and Savior, take a moment to let this truth settle into your heart. You may want to repeat this verse in first person in order to get it deep into your soul. "Blessed am I whose lawless deeds are forgiven, and whose sins are covered; blessed am I against whom You, Lord, no longer count my sin." Ask the Holy Spirit to lead you into all truth in this area.

Going forward as Christians we may fail, mess up, and not always keep God's law of love. However, grounded in I John 1:9, we can know that if we confess our sins the Father will *"cleanse us from all unrighteousness"* we amassed as a result of our compliance with sin. At the risk of redundancy I'll say this: His cleaning actually leaves us clean. And being clean in the area of sin is what justification is all about. So stand up in it, child of God; as unbelievable as it may seem, it is true. All praise and honor and glory forever to the Father who sought to bring us back into this justified state, and to Jesus our Savior for paying the price to get us here. You are justified—guiltless and declared innocent. Receive that today.

FORGIVEN

We may think we already know a thing or two about forgiveness. Doubtless we have had to learn about it at some point in a world full of darkness. However, as with justification, I'm going to ask you to ask the question: do I really get it? God's kind of forgiveness?

As if justification isn't stunning enough, forgiveness further reveals the unexplainable and miraculous act salvation really is. God forgives a man or woman who comes to Him and repents for every atrocity, for the worst slander, the simplest dismissal, and even the ugliest crimes against one another. It doesn't matter the degree to which we did or didn't do something; if we turn from our sin and confess Him as Lord, we are saved (Romans 10:9–10). What is the role of forgiveness in this whole thing? If justification takes away our sin, why does God seem to go one step further and bring forgiveness into the equation? Forgiveness, in the context of salvation, is a voluntary act in which God demonstrates He is going after more than just our cleanliness of sin.

Many religions of the world today get stuck on the same things as the Pharisees of Jesus' day. Jesus devoted time in His teachings to address their misdirected focus on the merely external appearance of holiness. In Matthew 23:25–28 for example, He refers to them as *"white washed tombs"* who were *"beautiful on the outside but on the inside. . . full of greed"* (NLT). Although God does not disregard holiness as He states in I Peter 1:16, *"be holy because I am holy,"* His holiness is not attained through the outward working and "ceremonies" the Pharisees were caught up on. Holiness before God comes through our relationship with Him made possible by the atoning work of Jesus on the cross. *"God made Him who had no sin to be sin for us, so that in Him we might become the righteousness of God"* (2 Corinthians 5:21, NLT) and there is simply no other way to be righteous and holy in God's sight than to be covered by the blood and righteousness of Christ! So as Justification deals with the sin situation in salvation, forgiveness' role is to deal with the *distance* our sin created between the Father and ourselves. Forgiveness, in essence, is what makes the relationship possible again after an offense has occurred.

Consider for a moment the word "forgive" in the Bible found in scriptures like Matthew 14:6 and I John 1:9. It is derived from the Greek word "aphiēmi"[8] and it literally means "to leave, to send away, or to let go." So when God says, "If we confess our sins He is faithful and just to forgive," we can read it this way: "He is faithful and just to [leave, send away, and let go of] our sins." Wow, feeling lighter at all? He is literally leaving our sins and offenses alone and even sending them away from our relationship with Him. How impossible is it to have a healthy, thriving relationship with someone you have not forgiven? Does that bitterness ever draw us close to someone? No, never. Bitterness is a driving and divisive force that seeks to hurt people on both ends of its clasp.

But in God's world He chooses to send the sin away instead of us. He reveals the priority of what He wants to have in closest proximity to Him.

God chooses to "begin again" with us because He knows the damage from our agreement with sin cannot be patched up—it has to be eradicated. At the end of all time, God will do one final sweep to rid the earth and all its inhabitants of evil once and for all. What a glorious day that will be! But for the time being He is working toward this eventual goal on a much more personal, individual level with the purpose that this redemptive work in individuals will steadily affect the whole. Justification clears the way for us to enter into heaven to live with God for eternity by clearing the penalty of sin over our lives. Forgiveness, likewise, is also a determining factor in our ability to be with God forever. But out of the two, forgiveness

---

8   Strong, James. (S.T.D, L.L.D) Strong's Exhaustive Concordance of the Bible, Royal Publishers INC. Nashville Tennessee.

is the one that makes fullness of life on earth in constant relationship with our Father possible. It is because of His forgiveness we can be welcomed back into His embrace. It is because He lets go of all the wrong done that we can come close to Him with confidence.

God's forgiving nature is what enables Him to remove our sins from us *"as far as the east is from the west"* (Psalm 103:12). It is through this aspect of His nature that He lets go of what is ugly in us to bring out what's most beautiful. He is calling us to embrace His forgiveness and not to shy away from it. You may think it is humility to think, "I am so not worthy" and to hold onto your sin, but it is not. It is a rejection of the Father's heart for you and it is often actually rooted in pride. This forgiveness is a gift to us, and pride often rejects a gift because it does not like the thought of receiving something it doesn't feel it earned! You didn't earn this, no one can. But we must receive it because of the love and graciousness of The Father. We must take Him at His word and arm ourselves against the lies of the enemy and even our own flesh that would seek to enslave us to shame and guilt. For the sake of the Father, we cannot allow it! Salvation, in its totality is the most concise display of the Father's love. Let the reality of the Father's forgiveness sink in. Confess any sin you may have not yet brought to Him and then receive the truth of His word for you in I John 1:9 and thank Him for the removal of any lingering shame from past sin. Do not allow the enemy to lie to you in this area. Ask the Holy Spirit for revelation of the Father's heart to you and your true state of righteousness before Him.

God forgives to set our relationship with Him free! Walk deeper into that freedom today!

ACCEPTANCE

We may be able to grasp the concepts of forgiveness and even justification surrounding salvation, but there is yet one more which may be the most astonishing of all. It is the fact that the moment we receive Jesus as the payment for our sin we are totally accepted by God. Since acceptance is such an elusive but sought after commodity in our society, we can think it quite a stretch to be fully accepted by a God whose very nature is Holy. But the Bible points to this truth that acceptance is possible for us all throughout its pages and no less here in Luke 15.

When we receive salvation we, like the son, return to the Father in repentance and recognition that we "have sinned against heaven and against" Him. This is true and a necessary step in our salvation. However, a problem arises if we get stuck on the concept of this next familiar phrase which, although we may not come out and say it, many of us feel in connection to our confession: "I am no longer worthy to be called your son. Make me like one of your hired servants." There it is, feel that? Have you ever felt that after confessing something to God? This is a classic example of how a twisted truth can support a lie. It is true that we are not worthy. We were not worthy of the pursuit and price Jesus Christ paid on the cross to buy us back from the power of darkness and slavery to sin. We are not *worthy* in ourselves of the love the Father pours upon us. The problem arises, however, when we try to apply the view of acceptance we have seen modeled in the world around us, to the heavenly exchange at salvation.

Many of us have felt the sting a lack of acceptance brings from certain crowds at school, work, social outings, or even the church. Any arena where God's ways and heart are not being represented will reinforce the worldview of acceptance to us orchestrated by the enemy of our souls and god of this world, the Devil. The devil's presentation of acceptance is talk the way I want you to, look the way I want you to, do what I want you to and you'll be accepted. It's based in control, built on conformity and runs on insecurity. The way of our Heavenly Father did not demand conformity and control but rather a plan that would take what made us unacceptable upon Himself through His Son to be forever done away with by His blood.

The father in the story of Luke 15 was not satisfied with having another servant to be left in the field. He ran out to his son and threw his arms around him as a complete, "Welcome home!" There was no penance to be paid. No work to be done in order for this son to earn his way back. It was a complete new start that the father was after and he moved quickly have some very significant garments placed on his son to cover him in his repentance. With these acts, the father not only extended his welcome back into his house, but assured the child of his continual welcome in his heart. Now remember, Jesus told this story to illustrate what happens in every story of a "sinner who repents." Faced with this truth, we have to let go of our insistence, "just make me like one of your hired hands," and receive what the Father wants for us which is to be His sons and daughters.

In Hebrews 4 we are taught to recognize that faith in Christ has become our "Sabbath rest" from trying to work our way back to the Father. *"For anyone who enters God's rest also rests from their works"* (Hebrews 4:10).

This chapter concludes with this thought: *"Let us then approach God's throne of grace with confidence, so that we may receive mercy and find grace to help us in time of need"* (v.16).

We can approach God "boldly" because of what Jesus our High Priest has accomplished for us (Hebrews 4:14–16, 5). This is possibly the greatest litmus test for what level of acceptance we feel we operate in with the Father. If there is fear in our approach to God, we have not been yet "perfected" in God's love because, *"perfect love drives out fear, because fear has to do with punishment. The one who fears is not made perfect in love"* (1 John 4:18). Although we rightly revere the Father, there should be no fear associated with our approach to God if we truly understand His love for us. Besides, how much room for fear did the father in Luke 15, an example of our Father, leave for fear in his relationship with his son?

Shame is another hindrance to receiving the acceptance portion of salvation. Pointing back to the truth found in justification in 1 John 1:9, we are assured that when we confess our sins, God has set it up that Christ not only forgives us but then "cleanses us from all wickedness." If we've been cleansed, and we have been, then there should be no lingering shame over what we've done. If our Lord forgets the sins we confess to Him (Hebrews 8:12) and we still feel bad about them, something has not translated correctly to us. The spirit of shame has to be dealt with to overcome its operation in our lives. As I learned from sermon years ago, shame convinces us we haven't just done something wrong but that we are wrong.[9] The enemy uses shame to convince us to hide like Adam and Eve did in the Garden of Eden after they discovered they were naked and in need of covering. The subtle lie of it all is that we cannot be fully cleansed and fully accepted by the Father. A key for being released from the lies and grip of shame is choosing to believe the truth about what God has said about us in His word.

> *There is therefore now no condemnation for those who are in Christ Jesus.*
>
> —Romans 8:1, ESV

Though we no doubt *feel* as this son did at the time, unworthy, we cannot stop there. Our Father doesn't and did not call us to work for Him; He has called us to be with Him. If we choose to remain in our unworthiness and reject what He has done, we will live below the calling we have as royal sons and daughters of the King. See, what we don't truly *know* inside as children of God *can* hurt us.

In the next section we're going to look at the specific items of clothing the father placed on his returned son and what they represent for us as dearly loved children of God our Father. Before we proceed, though, take a moment to ask the Holy Spirit to reveal to you any aspects of these truths that have not made it into your heart. If anything is revealed, go back and review what God has said about

---

9   "Shame" by Abi Stumvoll, BSSM First Year, Bethel Church, Redding, California, 2015-2016

you. Don't believe the lies anymore! You must receive the truth so that it can set you free!

Beloved, place yourself in this story and feel the Father's embrace of you because it is true for you as well. Jesus included this parable in the string of parables He was using to teach His listeners about the heart of the Father towards those lost in sin. God does not desire mere servants, He takes nothing less than Sons. Let Him pour on you his justice, forgiveness, and acceptance as you get ready to make sure you're wearing all the right clothing as one of His royal children.

REFLECTION QUESTIONS

1) After reading about Justification, Forgiveness, and Acceptance, were any sections hard for you to accept and receive for yourself? If so, how come?

    b) Take a moment to return to any of these sections you may have struggled with. Ask the Holy Spirit to help you and guide you into the Father's truth concerning you in this area.

2) How does it feel to be justified, forgiven, and accepted by God the Father? If you haven't already, take a few minutes to journal your response to this incredible offer from the Father. Be honest; it's okay if you are just beginning to believe it. Write a "thank you" note to the Father and tell Him what this revelation has meant to you. Be sure to listen for anything He may want to say back to you.

PART II

CHILDREN'S
CLOTHING...

HAVE YOU EVER EXPERIENCED THE AWKWARD SCENARIO WHEN someone buys you something to wear—or worse, *makes* you something you know is totally not your style? You gingerly accept it, trying to hide your dislike. After all, it's the thought that counts (and sometimes it's so bad you can't quite figure out what thought they could have had that you should be counting). But let's be honest. What happens to that garment or item as soon as you get home? It goes in the closet to be forgotten about until one day you discover it hasn't evaporated with time and now you have to find a way to discard it tastefully so that the giver never finds out.

When we become Christians, we're given many gifts, some of which are beautifully described as clothing by our text here in Luke 15. Unlike the scenario above, though, we don't usually shelve the "clothing" because we dislike it, but rather because of ignorance or disbelief. Many Christians are never made aware of the fullness of their salvation, or when presented with the extravagance of these gifts, they are unable to accept them.

We're about to examine the significance of each item the Father would like us to wear. Don't worry, His fashion sense is dead-on. He knows us inside and out and knows what we need.

As we go back into our story, place yourself in it as the son or daughter who has returned home to the father, and get ready to receive the children's clothing.

THE ROBE

F or me, new clothes are usually a welcomed luxury. I'm really not in need of any, I just really like them. If I find a reasonably priced piece of clothing or better yet a half-price sale, I just can't pass it up! But in the context of Luke 15, the new clothes presented by the father are more than a luxury, they are absolutely essential.

It's almost shocking how fast the father moves from the son's repentance into ensuring he is clean and dressed up. The son came to him looking tattered, worn, and smelling like pigs! The Father would have none of it. No son of His was going to remain looking like that.

The first item of clothing the Father calls for is a robe. Not just any robe—the *best* robe!

Zechariah 3 contains another story in the Bible where clothing seems very important. In this passage, Joshua represents the nation of Israel, which has fallen away from the Lord and been infiltrated by sin (Zechariah 3:8–9).

> *Then he showed me Joshua the high priest standing before the angel of the Lord, and Satan standing at his right side to accuse him. The Lord said to Satan, "The Lord rebuke you, Satan! The Lord, who has*

chosen Jerusalem, rebuke you! Is not this man a burning stick snatched from the fire?"

Now Joshua **was dressed in filthy clothes** *as he stood before the angel. The angel said to those who were standing before him,* **"Take off his filthy clothes.***" Then he said to Joshua, "See* **I have taken away your sin, and I will put fine garments on you.***"*

—Zechariah 3:1–4, NIV (emphasis added)

In this story, sin is represented by filthy clothes which prevented Joshua (symbolically Israel) from performing his rightful role as high priest of the Lord. In the same manner as the father commands his servants to get new clothes for his son (Luke 15:22), the angel of the Lord commands those standing before Joshua to take of his filthy clothes, making way for the rich garments of the Lord to be put on him.

In both Zechariah 3 and Luke 15, new garments are a sign of reinstatement and distinction. Elsewhere in the Bible, Jacob includes a change of clothes in the cleansing ceremony he holds for people in his household as they get ready to go to the place the Lord commanded him to go (Genesis 35:2).

We come to God wearing all of our bad deeds, unkind words and actions, repeated failures, baggage, deceit, pride, and cover-ups. We come with nothing to say for ourselves and no leverage to entice the Father to forgive us. We come to the cross clothed in our sin and return to the Father as children who lost their way and turned from Him.

Yet when we confess what we have done and declare we believe in and receive what Christ accomplished for us on the cross, our Father goes way beyond our request for mercy. He excitedly removes our defiled clothing and piles on us the luxuries of His kingdom. Our new robes contain favor and riches wrapped in love beyond measure.

Do not miss it, devalue it, or reject it. The Father has offered you His finest and He longs to put on you rich garments of forgiveness, righteousness, and wholeness. He has reinstated you to your original position and purpose in life—a child of God. The new garments are clean and enable you to stand in His presence. *"For God made Christ, who never sinned, to be the offering for our sin, so that we could be made right with God through Christ"* (2 Corinthians 5:21, NLT).

> *. . .and all who have been united with Christ in baptism have put on Christ, like putting on new clothes.*
>
> —Galatians 3:27, NLT

Picture the robe your Father wants to put on you. It's beautiful, soft, and luxurious and made of the finest linen. It's pure, it's lovely, and it's yours. Put it on and stand up tall and feel it drape over your shoulders and warm your heart. I know His love is extravagant—even unbelievable—but it's true, you are His and He's made this for you. Take a moment to sit in the Father's presence and thank Him for making you "white as snow" and for the "robe of righteousness" He has given you. There is no need for promises; He's not looking for you to tell Him how much better you'll do *for* Him. He wants you to receive what He's done *for* you. That, in turn, will change you from the inside out. You are clothed now with His garments, decorated by His favor and cleansed by His power. Wear it well, child. Wear His love with confidence. Like an old saying goes, "If it fits wear it." This robe indeed fits, child, it's made to.

> *I will rejoice greatly in the Lord My soul will exult in my God; for He has clothed me with garments of salvation, He has* **wrapped me with a robe of righteousness.**
>
> —Isaiah 61:10 (emphasis added)

THE RING

By now I hope you're enjoying the exquisite feel of the robe you're clothed in. Let's look at a second item of apparel the Father thought necessary for you: the ring. The father continues the adorning of His son by placing on his hand this well-known symbol of distinction and authority. Often a king or official would give a signet ring to someone he was instating into an office or position of authority. Pharaoh can be seen doing to Joseph when he puts him in charge of the whole land of Egypt (Genesis 41:42), and in Esther 8:2 the king is seen giving his ring to Mordecai when handing over to him the office and estate of Haman. In Luke 15, the father gives his son *a* ring of his own, not *his* ring. This symbolizes a certain type of authority as a son being delegated to him.

There is a scene from popular movie "A Knight's Tale" when William Thatcher's luck has run out while trying to attain his dream of being a knight. Born into a family of supposed poor descent, William is polarized from the honor of a knight simply because his family does not boast a royal heritage. With his head and arms fastened in gallows, he now awaits his punishment for pretending to be a knight so he could compete in the games. When the situation looks hopeless, an unassuming bystander uncovers his cloaked head to reveal himself as none other than the Black Prince of Wales, the only man powerful enough to release him. Until then the scene does not reveal whether the Prince is there to help or hinder William. However, in a climactic turn he has William released and proceeds to officially Knight him because of ancient royal descent found in William's family line. The Prince's word is above contestation and William is knighted.

When we come to Christ we are like William, without position and without any means of gaining it. We lost the position of dominion and authority given to us at creation (Genesis 1:28) when mankind sided with the devil in the fall (Genesis 3). Jesus Christ, however, came to *"destroy the works of the devil"* (I John 3:8) and He did just that when God raised Him from the dead. *"He (Christ) **disarmed the spiritual rulers and authorities**. He shamed them publicly by His victory over them on the cross"* (Colossians 2:15, NLT, emphasis added).

Jesus is our "Black Prince of Wales" but much, much more powerful.

Sometime back I was reading the gospels and marveling at the power and authority Jesus possessed as He walked the earth. Demons submitted to Him, all sickness fled from Him. After all, He was the Son of God. As I marveled at this I exclaimed, "Jesus I am amazed at your power."

Just then I felt Him answer me, "Now I want you to see yours..."

I looked down and realized I was on Luke 9:1 where Jesus called the twelve together and *"gave them power and authority to drive out all demons and cure diseases, and he sent them out to proclaim the kingdom of God and to heal the sick"*(NIV). Did you catch that? He gave *them* the power. I don't think there's a Christian alive who doesn't recognize Christ's power and authority, but just in case you need a little convincing have a look at Ephesians 1:19–22:

> *His incomparably great power for us who believe. That power is the same as the mighty strength He exerted when He raised Christ from the dead and seated Him* **at His right hand** *in the heavenly realms,* **far above all rule and authority, power and dominion, and every name that is invoked, not only in the present age but also in the one to come.** *And God placed* **all things under His feet…** (NIV, emphasis added)

Wow, that's authority and power far above ev-er-y-thing! Nothing matches Him and nothing is too great for Him. But here's the thing, scripture says *we* are seated in the exact same place *He* is in the heavenly places. *"And God **raised us up with Christ and seated us with Him in the heavenly realms in Christ Jesus**"* (Ephesians 2:6, emphasis added). If you read the rest of the chapter you'll realize the "us" in this verse is those who have been saved! Why is all this so important? Well, when Jesus died He reclaimed the authority stolen from man at The Fall. As we'll discover in the next section, His intended method of enforcing the victory at the cross would be through His church.

THE NAME OF JESUS

A very famous passage of scripture is Matthew 28:18–19 and it actually contains a revelation of authority often missed when reading it.

> *Then Jesus came to them and said, "All authority in heaven and on earth has been given to me. Therefore go make disciples of all nations, baptizing them in the name of the Father and of the Son and of the Holy Spirit."* (NIV)

Here, Jesus approaches His disciples after His glorious victory on the cross. He starts out by saying "**all authority** has been given to me." This is great for Jesus and if He stopped there we, the church, would never have to worry about the implications of what He was about to say next. Without the "therefore" these two statements would seem fairly disconnected; Jesus says, "I've got all the authority" (wow, that's great, Jesus)…"you guys go teach people"… huh? But what He's saying here is not disconnected at all! In fact it is completely connected. I remember a Sunday school lesson when my pastor pointed out that whenever you see the word "therefore" in scripture you have to pay attention to what was said before it because it essentially means, "because of this" or "because of what I just said." So if we apply this to our passage it would read, "All authority…has been given to me (and because of this)…go" Or in other words, "because I have all the authority, you guys go and make disciples." A little later in this passage He reveals how this is all supposed to work: *"baptizing them **in the name of** the Father and of the Son and of the Holy Spirit"* (v. 19).

To look at this further we have to go to John 16:23–24, where Jesus instituted a new way of praying:

> *…in that day you will no longer ask me anything. Very truly I tell you, my Father will give you whatever you ask in my name.* **Until now**

you have not asked for anything in my name. *Ask and you will receive, and your joy will be complete.* (NIV, emphasis added)

Scripture supports the use of the Name of Jesus in Mark 16:17–18 and Matthew 18:19–20. What's in a name? I like what Andrew Murray says about this:

> What is a person's name? It is a word or expression in which a person is represented to us. When I mention, or hear a name, it brings to mind the whole man, what I know of him, and also the impression he has made on me. The name of a king includes his honor, his power, and his kingdom. His name is the symbol of his power. And so each name of God embodies and represents some part of the glory of the Unseen One. The Name of Christ is the expression of everything He has done and everything He is and lives to do as our Mediator.[10]

To come "in the name of" someone is to come "by the authority of" or on behalf of someone.[11] Andrew Murray expounded upon the meaning of this phrase in reference to Christ by stating to come in His name is to "come with his power and authority as

---

10 Andrew Murray, "With Christ in the School of Prayer" chp.24 cited from worldinvisible.com/library/murray

11 "In the name of" Merriam-Webster.com. 2017. https://merriam-webster.com (accessed May 13, 2017)

his representative and substitute." When Christ gave us His name to use, He authorized us to come with His power and authority on His behalf. Christ's name is above all names and His name represents who He is. It is through our relationship with Him that we can be confident we can do the things which require His authority in His name.

For us to use His name with confidence, we must have complete identification with Christ within us. We must know the truth of Galatians 3:27 that we *"have been baptized into Christ."* Another meaning is immersed. We have been immersed into Christ and the lives we live, we live in Christ (Galatians 2:20).

It's important for believers to realize the authority we have in Christ, not only for the defensive but also the offensive. This authority is our legs to stand on in a fight. The enemy of our souls comes to *"kill, steal and destroy"* (John 10:10, NIV). Many times, he is given the ability to do so in our lives because we simply do not know our ability and responsibility to overcome him. When we resist him in the name of Christ, the devil and all the powers of darkness must flee. They must bow to Christ because He has already defeated them (Colossians 2:15). Many Christians spend a lot of time being beat up by a defeated and disarmed opponent. If we do not recognize what Christ has won for us, we will stay beneath the stuff we are actually *"seated above"* (Ephesians 2:6). We need to recognize the power behind the statement we all too often just tag on to the end of our prayers. "In the name of Jesus" is an inward revelation based on our relationship with Christ that produces faith in us to believe in what Christ has accomplished. The power is not in the phrase itself. You will begin to experience the power of the One who backs the use of

His name when you step out in faith and take up your position as a child of God authorized to come on behalf of the Exalted Son of God—Jesus. He has the power; believe Him and bravely push back the darkness.

THE SANDALS

Now, if you are male please don't skip this part (this is not the "girl" chapter!). Because there's plenty here for you. However, please allow me a paragraph or so to rave about shoes!

No outfit is complete without the right pair of shoes. Ladies, can I get an amen? Not much is mentioned about these sandals given to this returning son. Given the fact that his wealthy father brought him the best of everything else, I'm sure they too were quite something. Oh how good this son must have felt getting to put on those sandals after pounding on hard ground for who knows how long during his journey back to the Father. Finally, his feet could rest on the protective material of sandals made *just* for him. This isn't a scene from Cinderella where they bring out some generic sandal and everyone holds their breath hoping it will fit! No, these sandals are *made for him*. They slip right on, instantly relieving the discomfort of his former walk of life.

As I've read the many commentaries regarding this passage in preparation for this book, one thing they all agree on is that servants did not wear sandals—only sons did. Being a shoe lover, I was thrilled at the opportunity to study shoes in the Bible...now you're talking, Holy Spirit! I will however restrain myself and give you a brief summarization of shoes in the Bible. Though there were many uses of footwear in the Bible, they were most often worn by people of recognition, such as officials or soldiers just like in 1 King 2:5. Expensive sandals, like the one this son is wearing here, were always a status symbol (Song of Songs 7:1). The Father continues to deck out His son with all the status of His kingdom.

In Ephesians 6:15, Paul encourages the believer to have something on their feet. *"For shoes, put on the peace that comes from the Good News so that you will be fully prepared"* (NLT). This verse is placed within the context of the armor of God the believer is supposed to be wearing (see Ephesians 6:13–18). Evidently, the Peace of God we are figuratively to put on our feet is protective in some manner. Most parents indicate concern for their children's feet when their children go out to play, exclaiming, "Put your shoes on!"—especially if they're going to be playing on the sidewalk or rough ground. Why? They don't want them to cut themselves, slip, or fall. Whatever the case may be, the rockier the terrain the better the shoes must be. As one who has jammed my tender toes into the most ridiculous styles of four-inch heals known to man, only to be in pain about an hour later, I've grown to appreciate a good pair of sensible shoes.

Children of God, we must have "our shoes on" when walking the battlefield of life. According to Ephesians 6:15 that footgear is to be the *"peace that comes from the Good News!"* So wait, peace? That's it? You may be surprised to know that out of all the battle armor imagery laid out in this passage, peace is considered among them. Not just any peace, but the peace that comes from the gospel. I like how the Amplified Bible illuminates this: *"and having strapped on your feet the gospel of peace in preparation (to face the enemy with firm-footed stability and the readiness produced by the good news)."* Knowing the peace we have with God through the gospel makes us "firm-footed" in our walk of life. When we walk in the knowledge of who we are in Christ, we walk in great strength to stand against all the forces that may come against us. Knowing we are welcomed in our Father's house and receiving all He has won for us, assurance of His acceptance, and hope in our glorious future in Him, gives us one of the most powerful weapons we can have as Christians—peace! From this position we can fight and we will win. Clothed in all the extravagance our Father designed for us, we can stand tall as sons and daughters adorned in His strength.

Take some time to review the clothing you're now wearing as a child of God. Thank Father for every item He's given you and let the revelation contained within each show you the love the Father has for you. Let His peace wash over you and strengthen you. "Child, put your shoes on!" and don't ever let anything or anyone take them off.

See what great love the Father has lavished on us, that we should be called children of God! And that is what we are!

—I John 3:1, NIV

OFFENSIVE GRACE

There are some sizable cultural differences, in Luke 15, between the audiences of Jesus' day and today that may cause us to miss some key lessons Jesus is after. For starters, sons receiving an inheritance from their fathers the way they did at the time of this text is drastically different from common practice today. Unfortunately our culture today often thinks little past our own lifetime and the current state of the average family debt makes the thought of leaving inheritance for children or children's children seem increasingly hopeless. Furthermore, in western culture, children are encouraged to be independent from their families and often expected to be pursuing their own careers to provide for themselves by the time they reach young adulthood. The idea that sons would wait on an inheritance from their fathers doesn't connect with us. To get what's going on in this story, we need to understand what this story would have meant to the avid listeners.

The Bible paints quite a picture of this intemperate younger son. Jesus introduces him by his presumptuous demand for his father to give him his inheritance, which was no small request according to the laws of this culture. This demand would have been like saying, "I wish you were dead already!" Jesus swiftly moves on to describe the rebellious and lascivious lifestyle this son lived. Rebellion like this from a son was dealt with very severely; in fact, it was punishable by death according to Deuteronomy 21:18–21. The hearers would have certainly gasped at the attitude and actions this son displayed. Not only that, they would have been very confused by the father's decision to give his son what he was demanding. It was possible for a father to designate an inheritance to a son before he died, but it would not go into effect until after the father died. So the son was not to use it or sell it until then. The son in our story takes what's been given and spends it straight away without thought of this clause. Something else is also being brought up here by Jesus' story. The crowd would have been dumbfounded by the father's apparently permissive parenting. They would not have identified with him actually allowing such an offence in his family. He would have appeared very lax, weak, and even stupid to allow this disobedience to continue.

The listeners would have begun to feel a little bit better upon hearing the misfortunes and eventual consequences the son seemed to run into along the road of his life. They would have felt much more justified by about verse 15, concluding he was getting what he rightfully deserved. It is true sin will always take you from the blessing of the Father's house into some nasty pigsty of the earth. The hearers would have expected the story to end with the son in the pigpen getting what he deserved for his life of sin. But just as everyone is feeling happier about the story, Jesus throws in a massive curveball. The son has a moment of clarity and makes a decision to return to his father's house to work for him. Return to his father's house *after* he's blown his inheritance (which again was punishable by death). At this point they would have been on the edge of their seats awaiting the son's fate as he returns home. Surely he'll get what he deserves! If this father had any regard at all for the law he would do what was right and have this son punished! But then...Jesus leaves the minds of these listeners, so heavily steeped in religion, confounded as he presents the father's reaction as one of total grace, forgiveness, and acceptance towards this son. In a culture that so valued obedience in children, Jesus presents an exchange between an unruly son and unbelievably gracious father that would have been inconceivable—beyond belief, not to mention incredibly offensive.

So what was Jesus up to? Was he just recounting one of his favourite stories completely oblivious to the reception he would get from his listeners? I think not—Jesus knew exactly what He was doing! At the beginning of chapter 15 in Luke, we get insight into what started Jesus on the series of rants to which this parable offers a brilliant conclusion.

> *Now the tax collectors and sinners were all gathering around to hear Him (Jesus).* **But the Pharisees and the teachers of the law muttered, "This man welcomes sinners and eats with them.***"*
>
> —Luke 15:1–2, NIV (emphasis added)

This triggered something in Jesus and he decided to go after it hard with three parables' worth of material. In this portion of Luke we see a literary device called an "inclusio" which begins at verse 24 and ends at verse 32. An inclusio is when writers "bracket off" a section of writing by placing similar material at both the beginning and end of that section. This is used to highlight a main theme or, in this case, a climactic issue of the text. The writer of this passage intentionally places an inclusio in our scripture in order to highlight a main theme. This occurs when Jesus begins to describe the elder brother's role in this story.

> **"For this son of mine was dead and is alive again; he was lost and is found."** *So they began to celebrate. Meanwhile, the older son was in the field and as he came near the house he heard music*

and dancing. So he called one of the servants and asked him what was going on. "Your brother has come", he replied, "and your father has killed the fattened calf because he has him back safe and sound." The older brother became angry and refused to go in, so his father went out and pleaded with him join the celebration.

But he answered his father, "Look! All these years I've been slaving for you and never disobeyed your orders. Yet you never gave me even a young goat so I could celebrate with my friends. But when this son of yours who has squandered your property with prostitutes comes home you kill the fattened calf for him!"

"My son," the father replied, "you are always with me and everything I have is yours. But we had to celebrate and be glad, because **this brother of yours was dead and is alive again; he was lost and is found.**"

—Luke 15:24–32, NIV (emphasis added)

In reaction to the Pharisees and teachers of the law, Jesus decides to convey a story which contrasts a son, the worst of "sinners," receiving grace and welcoming from his father who was foolishly gracious according to them. The older son was completely focused on the "rules" and earning his place in the father's house. At this point, Jesus wants them to see themselves in this story. He is hoping they will catch the similarities between the elder brother and their perceptions of how the kingdom works and their attitudes toward sinners who are graciously welcomed home by the Father. He is in essence saying, you are the elder brother and those *"sinners"* I allow to eat with me are the younger son.

ELDER SON ISSUES

So what are some of the lessons Jesus is hoping the Pharisees will catch in this story? Keeping in mind this whole string of parables was prompted by the Pharisees' disapproval of Jesus' tendency to "eat with sinners," we can see this story is meant in part to reveal and combat certain beliefs that would serve as precursors to self-righteousness and competition in the family of God.

During the father's gentle, consoling speech to His eldest son (after finding him sitting outside, pouting), he says, "You are **always with me** and **everything I have is yours**." The father attempts to deflect his son's gaze from the current situation by reminding him of what he already had available to him. The father is speaking to a heart issue revealed in the son's complaint. "All these years

> Everything I have is yours.

I've been **slaving for you** and never disobeyed your orders!" This son saw his relationship with the father as a lot of work with very little reward.

The Pharisees knew this pattern of relating to God very, very well. They were part of the group given spiritual charge over the people for the 400-year span between the Old and New Testament. Throughout this period they had managed to enslave the people to rules and laws that went way beyond the original law of God. In their view of God, His affection had to be earned and His punishment warded off by keeping the law (plus the additional laws *they* created!).

Under this way of thinking, anyone who did not comply with the law deserved separation from God. But even if all the requirements of the law were fulfilled by an individual, this system still offered a great deal of distance from the Holy One. In the Parable of the Lost Son, Jesus begins modeling an offensive grace to a community who had no real idea what it meant to be a child of God. He was foreshadowing the restoration movement of sinners to sons which He would usher in through His death and resurrection. The grace the father extended to the younger son offended his elder son in the same way it would have offended the Pharisees and keepers of the law. At this point, however, Jesus is hoping they will catch the heart of the Eternal Father concerning true salvation.

The religious system of Jesus' audience had created a view of God as a master instead of a good Father. It limited how close they could get to God as well as what they believed was available from Him. Jesus is correcting both of these ideologies in the father's answer, "I am always with you" and "Everything I have is yours." Think about this last one. Everything I, God of the Universe and creator of all, have is yours! Whoa…all along this older son had access to all his father had, so it makes his request for one calf and a less than spectacular party a little short-sighted (Luke 15:29). In reality, he had access to not just one calf but every calf his father owned! So what robbed him all those years of all the fun he could have been having? The elder son *chose* to live as a servant in his father's house rather than a son. He, like the Pharisees, thought working *for* the father would earn him the rewards *from* the father he so desperately desired. "I've slaved for you…" This is how the world operated around them and religion was part of that system. When you work for someone you feel a certain measure of entitlement. As an employee, you're entitled pay for the hours you work. This is largely how our world system also works today. But here in this parable, Jesus opposes these mindsets and starts to show both his audience then and us today a revelation about Father God.

Everything the younger son received from the father when he returned home came from his father's immense grace and goodwill. The elder son really had nothing to lose from the benevolence his dad showed his wayward sibling! The father did not have to take from the older to give to the younger (for there is always more than enough in God's kingdom) so no part of his inheritance would have been at stake. The sad part was that the elder son was jealous of what his younger sibling was able to receive from the father because he didn't realize he had actually taken himself out of all the blessings that were his because of ignorance about who he was.

In Hebrews 4:10, the writer speaks of a "rest" made available to all who receive salvation through faith in Jesus Christ's work on the cross. *"There remains a Sabbath rest for the people of God for anyone who enters God's rest also rests from his own work"* (NIV). Hebrews 4:3 clarifies who enters that rest: *"Now we who have believed enter that rest"* (NIV).

Receiving in full what Christ has done results in a deep rest in our walk with God. Rest from working to try earn any aspects of our salvation by our own effort. In salvation we start out leaning entirely on the grace of God and the sacrifice of Jesus but then subtly we can become less and less convinced that we really are children of God and that all the benefits we receive are truly secured. We may find ourselves working again to earn the Father's love and many blessings. A rap sheet of perfect church attendance, sufficient good works, clean living, and a string of ministries you've served may impress your pastor, but it is not solely what your Heavenly Father desires.

Jesus' parable presents two sons who represent two groups of individuals. The younger represents all sinners fallen short of God's glory and needing his forgiveness, while the older stands in for all who "earned" salvation under an old system about to be made obsolete and had never been able to see themselves as children of God. As the story unfolds we witness the father, representing the Heavenly Father, relating to each child uniquely and seeking to adjust the way both perceive themselves and what life is truly like in His household.

These are the precious revelations He wants his children to receive today. Although we no longer relate directly to the Pharisees since we now receive salvation through Jesus, we do tend to see ourselves and others in the kingdom through their cloudy lenses. God has made incredible and extravagant grace available to those who, by faith, will receive it from Him. We never deserved this honor to be sons and daughters, but we must fully receive it to live in the fullness of relationship and power the Father desires for us. Like the elder brother, jealousy or self-righteousness we may experience towards others has been rooted in a failure to recognize who we are and what we have in Him—children who have access to everything of His!

God offers a call to the Pharisees in this parable to rest from their labour and come and be His children. In the coming chapters we will discuss and explore servanthood in the life of sons and daughters of God, but right now I'm hoping to set up the right platform in your heart from which all service to God must take place. It is from the restful position of dearly loved sons and daughters that we return his love and walk with Him, enjoying all He has made available to us.

THE CELEBRATION

*"We **had** to celebrate!"*

—Luke 15:32 (emphasis added)

To the father, celebrating his lost son's return was simply the right thing to do. The celebration was a must! Interestingly, there is also quite a bit of celebration in Jesus' teaching before this parable (Luke 15:6, 9, 24). With so much emphasis on partying it up after something or someone lost gets found, Jesus is subtly introducing one last perspective of Heaven to his listeners currently stuck in religiosity. While Jesus had already laid out a pretty offensive position on salvation to His observers, now within His deliberate description of the celebration He strides into an even greater depth of wonder at the unthinkable reality of grace in the Father's plan of salvation.

After the younger son's return and swift restoration, everybody begins to party.

> *"'Bring the fattened calf and kill it. Let's have a feast and celebrate. For this son of mine was dead and is alive again; he was lost and is found.' So they began to celebrate."*

—Luke 15:23–24, NIV

That's it, the party begins! Heaven moves on! The father invites all his friends to make a very important transition in how they relate to this son. A distinction has been made between how he was viewed and how he will be viewed from now on. Before—dead and lost, now—alive and found. The son had a whole new image from Heaven's viewpoint. The Bible echoes this image change later through Paul when he implores his readers to recognize the one who has repented and accepted Christ as their Savior as a completely *"new creation"* (2 Corinthians 5:17, NIV).

If you viewed the son's return home the way the elder brother did, you too would be confused about the quick and reckless decision to celebrate. The elder son viewed salvation as so much work to keep and retain the rewards of being a child of God that there really wasn't reason to celebrate. Jesus is foreshadowing the incredible burden He would remove through His death and resurrection from the backs of erring children wishing to return home. The system was about to change drastically from arduous law-keeping to a faith-based reliance grace poured out by the Father. This grace would make it possible for all mankind to walk rightly with Him through the power of His Spirit within them. This, most certainly, was something to celebrate! Jesus graciously and lovingly is trying to get his audience to see the joy true salvation would bring if they would but receive it.

The father throwing a feast indicates something wonderful has happened. Celebrations take place when something is finished, restored, and/or accomplished. All three of these events occur the moment someone receives Christ. An old life is finished, a new life full of the blessings as children of God begins, and another soul is brought to safety and fullness within the welcoming presence of the Father.

Have you ever had a really great party thrown for you? Not a lame one like the kind where you don't really know anyone and can't figure out why that guy from down the street is raiding your fridge. Can you remember a time where you felt especially honored like a graduation, birthday, anniversary, or work promotion? Well, whether you have or not, think about this: the day you returned to the Father, **all** of heaven celebrated you! God, Jesus, the Holy Spirit, all the angels and saints who have gone before you, everyone partied the day you came home. Heaven celebrates you! And if you asked the Father why, He would answer you as simply and tenderly He did those in Luke 15, "Because you were dead and I wanted you alive, you were lost and now you are found!" He pursued you. He considers you valuable—so valuable He was willing to give His life to get to you. You mean everything to Him! A celebration marks the end of something and beginning of something new. In this case the end of an old identity and the re-establishment of the true one. Once justification, forgiveness, and acceptance have occurred simultaneously through the decision to receive Him, it is truly time to party and since salvations occur daily, heaven must be a place of continuous celebration! In the celebration our restoration is completed, our acceptance is displayed, and we are established as a new creation. The victory over sin is thoroughly celebrated and then we move on into kingdom life. Whatever you were is forgotten and the focus shifts to who you are.

After the father's heart-to-heart talk, the elder son's reaction is not recorded in this passage. It is possible Jesus gives room for

His audience to consider their own heart responses to the revelation He has conveyed to them. Will they join Him in rejoicing over the transformation of sinners to sons? Will they gain His perspective on what is truly being made available to them and let go of their self-righteous attempts at earning the favor of God?

Heaven truly partied the day you came home and continues to celebrate your journey forward. Salvation restored our position as sons and daughters of God, reactivated our destinies, and gave us eternal hope in a glorious future! Jesus made it possible to receive within us the presence of His Holy Spirit as our comforter, empowering us to walk in holiness and power doing what Jesus did on the earth (Galatians 5:24–25, John 14:12). Salvation brought to us healing (Isaiah 53:5, I Peter 2:24).

What the work of Christ accomplished both in Heaven and earth truly is a reason to celebrate. If you haven't yet personally rejoiced in the salvation you have received, or if it's just been a while, go ahead and throw a party! Spend time meditating on what the Father thinks about you and thank Him for all He has done. Join the celebration whatever that looks like for you—perhaps worship through song, journaling, prayer, or even dancing in the joy of the Lord. Whatever it is, ask Holy Spirit to fill you with even greater joy in your salvation as you fully embrace your identity as a child of God! Celebrate with Him because He absolutely had to celebrate you.

PART III

DEVOTED SONS
AND DAUGHTERS

Until now we've been working through the truth of scripture regarding the position of Sons and Daughters of God. I hope you've had many encounters with the Father and experienced His love and confirmation of the truth in your hearts. The revelation of our identity is central to our lives as Christians. Without it, we will inevitably end up striving at a distance from the Father, failing to enjoy the life He desires for us to have with Him.

I'm going to shift gears a little and start to speak to the important "other side" of this issue. A fear exists within the body of Christ that sometimes keeps us resistant to the full understanding of our immense privileges as children of God. This fear is based in the belief that too much emphasis on grace or our position as Sons could produce a licence to sin or disregard God's holiness. There are many false grace messages blowing through the body of Christ seeking to distort its view of God and consume the lie that living like the world is true freedom. The next section is not meant to address false teachings in their entirety, but we will go to

> After all, royalty should act like royalty.

the scriptures to find the heart of the Father on the conduct of His children. After all, royalty should act like royalty.

A LICENCE TO SIN?

THERE ARE MANY STORIES ABOUT WAYWARD PRINCES OR PRINCESSES who decide to dismiss their responsibilities to the kingdom in favor of a licentious lifestyle pleasing to their own desires. Living as royalty is challenging and does come with innate responsibilities wrapped up in the reality that life is no longer your own (I Corinthians 6:19–20).

The Apostle John wrote the book of First John during a time when a teaching called Gnosticism was starting to creep into the church. Gnosticism challenged many foundational teachings of Christ, one of which was that all matter including the body was evil. This led to the confusion that since matter itself was evil—and not the breaking of God's laws—breaking His law was of no moral consequence.[12] John, writing to address the misuse of freedom found in Gnostic teachings threatening to take his congregation off track, writes:

---

12 NIV Study notes, Introduction to 1 John, Gnosticism

> ...*God is light, and in Him is no darkness at all. If we say we*
> *have fellowship with Him while we walk in darkness, we lie and do*
> *not practice truth. But if we walk in the light, as He is in the light,*
> *we have fellowship with one another, and the blood of Jesus his Son*
> *cleanses us from all sin.*

—I John 1:5–7, ESV

John admonishes his readers to "walk in the light" which he later qualifies as an exhortation to abstain from sinful behavior as royal children of God. As Christians, we know we are not *supposed* to sin, but why? What is sin and why does God desire we stay clear of it? Paul, one of the greatest advocates in the Bible for Sonship and justification through faith, thought it important to pose a question to his newly freed converts to Christ: *"**Should** we go on sinning that grace may abound?"* (Romans 6:1, NIV, emphasis added) There are many messages about grace floating around in the church today that seem to ask this same question. Indeed, because of God's immeasurable gift to us through His Son, we now live under grace as children of God. Because of this grace, lightning bolts will likely not strike us the moment we sin, but the question posed here is not *could* we sin, but *should* we sin?

Apart from an obvious answer, if we're honest, sin rarely, if ever, offers any wholesome benefit to ourselves or the lives of those around us. Additionally and most importantly is the effect sin has on us and our relationship to the Father. The word translated "sin" comes from the Greek word "hamartanó" and literally means, "I miss the mark." It was frequently used in ancient times when an archer would miss his target. In essence, it means to make a mistake or do, think, or speak something that misses the mark of God's holiness. But there are a few scriptures which offer another perspective on sin and may help reveal further why the Father desires His children stay away from it.

Hebrews 12:1 says, *"Therefore, since we are surrounded by such a huge crowd of witnesses to the life of faith, let us strip off every **weight that slows us down, especially the sin that so easily trips us up"** (NLT, emphasis added). The author of this passage emphatically describes sin as an arduous weight or entanglement to the child of God. It has the potential to interfere with the race we're running in the good destiny our God has designed for us. In short, we were meant to run unhindered and we've been given the power and freedom to do so. Agreeing with a sin of any kind allows it to be an obstacle in our path.

Also, when Jesus came He fulfilled the requirements of the Old Testament Law and enacted the New Covenant. Jesus, shockingly, introduced a new law with an entirely different foundation— Love. In Matthew 26:36–40, Jesus takes all of the commandments the law ever gave right up until His time and boils them down to two simple commands He felt were sufficient to cover everything:

> *Love the Lord Your God with all your heart, all your soul, and all your mind. This is the first and greatest commandment. A second is equally important; Love your neighbor as yourself. The entire law and all the demands of the prophets are based on these two commandments.* (NLT)

Love God. Love others. Love yourself.

Jesus said if you focused on doing this, you would fulfill all the requirements of any of the laws of righteousness. If we think about it honestly, is there any sinful action that benefits others, shows love to them, or does not hurt yourself and/or others? Let's take stealing for example; we know it's wrong, but *why* is it wrong? Well, is stealing loving? Does the one who is stolen from feel loved? Does it benefit them? And in the end does it really benefit the one who has stolen? It may for a while, but sooner or later the consequences to these actions will come. And, most importantly, is stealing from others showing love for God? Are we displaying any honor to Him or others if we steal from them? Does stealing show trust in God to provide? Sin in all its various forms is always a violation against love. Love for God, love for others, and/or love for ourselves. And when we step out of love in any area of our life we begin to incur the consequences of the loveless world in which we live.

Another problem with sinning as children of God is that when we become aware of sin, we often entertain an opportunistic entity called shame. Shame forces us into hiding just like our ancestors Adam and Eve following their first agreement with sin (Genesis 3:1–10). Shame knows exactly what lies to speak to us. Shame reveals our "nakedness" and causes us to become entirely aware of our failures, but unlike grace, offers no answer for them. Shame attacks our identity and instead of saying, "You've done

> Sin in all its various forms is always a violation against love.

something bad," it says, "You are something bad!" It drives us away into a place far from our Father and inundates us with lies about Him. It is this distance from Him, and the potential for our destruction it brings, that the Father wants to save us from. The safest place we can be as Royals is in the palace with the protection of our Father and His armies. Shame can be dealt with and disarmed if we come to know the truth about sin and what Father has made available to us.

Paul spent ample time talking about sin, and a great deal of his teachings on the subject can be found in Romans chapters 6 to 8. One of the major points he makes to his readers throughout his teachings is that if they choose to obey sin they become *slaves to sin* and sin takes away their freedom (Romans 6:16). And he emphasizes that a believer is no longer a slave to sin because of the new nature given to them through salvation (Romans 6:6–7). After salvation, we become *the righteousness of God in Christ Jesus* (2 Corinthians 5:21) and *the righteous requirements of the law* are *fulfilled in us* (Romans 8:4).

What does all this mean? Well, apart from being insanely good news, it all points to a significant identity change for the believer. Although we've already looked at our new identity in part earlier, now we're going to see it in the context of sin. As Paul demonstrates in I Corinthians 6, our perspective on sin itself should change drastically in light of the salvation we've received.

> *Or do you not know that the unrighteous will not inherit the kingdom of God? Do not be deceived: neither the sexually immoral, nor idolaters, nor adulterers, nor men who practice homosexuality, nor thieves, nor the greedy, nor drunkards, nor revilers, nor swindlers will inherit the kingdom of God. And such* **were** *some of you. But you were washed, you were sanctified, you were justified in the name of the Lord Jesus Christ and by the Spirit of our God.*
>
> —I Corinthians 6:9–11, ESV (emphasis added)

Did you catch a twist in this passage? The first part lists sins as identities—the sexually immoral, thieves, drunkards, etc., indicating these particular groups of people were identified by their sin. But in verse 11 Paul makes a very important distinction: "such *were* some of you. *But...*"! Contained within this verse is a crucial perspective on the sufficient work of Christ. Paul is saying at one time you were considered part of this ugly list of those who could not enter a place like heaven, which is the very dwelling place of God and all His holiness. But, "you *were* **washed**, you were **sanctified**, you were **justified** in the name of the Lord Jesus Christ and by the Spirit of our God" (emphasis added).

When we receive the sacrifice of Christ and welcome God's Spirit into our hearts, everything about us changes. We are no longer identified by our sin. We are identified by Christ, washed, sanctified and justified. It's truly amazing! In essence, sin is separated from us.

Paul talks about sin in the same fashion describing it as something separate from himself that works within him:

> *For I do not understand my own actions. For I do not do what I want, but I do the very thing I hate. Now if I do what I do not want, I agree with the law, that it is good. So now* **it is no longer I who do it, but sin that dwells within me**.
>
> —Romans 7:17, NLT (emphasis added)

Why is it important to make the distinction? If we define ourselves as sinners, we'll likely keep on doing what sinners do... sin. But Paul knew better than to define himself by the sin he was struggling with, which is why he could write confidently that there is *"now no condemnation for those who are in Christ"* (Romans 8:1). Paul is exhorting his readers both then and today to realize Christ truly had changed everything for them. They were, and likewise we are, no longer *"slaves to the power of sin"* (Romans 6:5–14).

> *Sin is no longer your master, for you no longer live under the requirements of the law. Instead, you live under the freedom of God's grace.*
> —Romans 6:14, NLT

You are not your sin, and because of Christ and the power of the Holy Spirit in you, you are not in bondage to the power of sin either! Whenever sin comes at us, we can confess it to the Father and nail it to the cross of Christ where He dealt with it forever. *"Those who belong to Christ Jesus have nailed the passions and desires of their sinful nature to his cross and crucified them there"* (Galatians 5:24, NLT).

In doing this we choose to believe the truth about ourselves that we are no longer considered "sinners" but sons and daughters of God, given a new nature in Christ. When we acknowledge and agree with the truth, we access the power to overcome by His Spirit and disempower whatever lie sin is tempting us with. Agreement with the truth will always disempower a lie.

> Agreement with the truth will always disempower a lie.

Attached to every temptation is a lie about who we are and who God the Father is. Just as with Eve in the Garden of Eden, the Devil uses sin to try to drive a wedge into our relationship with our Father. Outside the protection knowing the truth about Him and

79

ourselves provides, we become entangled and weighed down, unable to run like we should! Sin just does not *fit* a child of God.

Inevitably we forget who we are from time to time and allow ourselves to agree with temptation, anger, lust, envy, etc., but if and when we do, we have an "advocate" who intercedes for us. *"My little children, I am writing these things to you so that you may not sin. But if anyone does sin, we have an advocate with the Father, Jesus Christ the righteous"* (1 John 2:1, ESV).

We do not have to live under the effects of sin and we must not confuse condemnation with conviction. Once a sin is dealt with, confessed and repented of, the Father remembers it no more. Any further condemnation you hear over that sin is not His voice! Moving on in the freedom His grace has provided will give us the ability to properly clean up any mess we may have made and any way others may have been affected by our sin. The Christian life is less about trying not to sin and more about becoming who we truly are. Sin should not be the focus of our lives—sonship is.

In this same passage of Romans 6 to 8, Paul spends a great deal of time elaborating on the beauty of grace. He tells us grace has enabled us to overcome the power of sin. We are no longer "slaves" to it! Because of what Christ has done, we no longer "have to" sin. The grace we have received as children of God is in no way a licence to sin. In fact it's quite the opposite. It is the freedom not to.

So, how is this glorious victory over sin enforced in our lives? Fortunately, Paul also shared about this: it is through the Holy Spirit, God's Spirit, within us.

You, however, are not in the flesh but in the Spirit, if in fact the Spirit of God dwells in you. Anyone who does not have the Spirit of Christ does not belong to him. But if Christ is in you, although the body is dead because of sin, the Spirit is life because of righteousness.

—Romans 8:9–10, ESV

When we receive Christ as our Savior, the Bible tells us the Holy Spirit indwells us. The Holy Spirit is God's Spirit and His nature and attributes dwell on the inside of us. That is why aspects of His character will be seen through us, such as *"love, joy, peace, patience, kindness, goodness, faithfulness, gentleness and self-control"* (Galatians 5:22–23, NLT).

Paul is talking about the fulfillment of the new covenant prophecy found in Jeremiah 31:33–34:

For this is the covenant that I will make with the house of Israel after those days, declares the Lord: I will put my law within them, and I will write it on their hearts. And I will be their God, and they shall be my people. And no longer shall each one teach his neighbor and each his brother, saying, "Know the Lord," for they shall all know me, from the least of them to the greatest, declares the Lord. For I will forgive their iniquity, and I will remember their sin no more. (ESV)

God was prophesying that an entirely new relationship between his people and Himself would come. With that, the process of sanctification would switch from outward to inward. Some more new covenant language offers even more insight into the nature of the new relationship:

And I will give you a new heart, and a new spirit I will put within you. And I will remove the heart of stone from your flesh and give you a heart of flesh. And I will put my Spirit within you, and cause you to walk in my statutes and be careful to obey my rules.

—Ezekiel 36:26–27, ESV

Paul in Romans 8 is now reiterating this relationship, except he is talking in the past tense:

For God has done what the law, weakened by the flesh, could not do. By sending his own Son in the likeness of sinful flesh and for sin, he condemned sin in the flesh, in order that the righteous requirement of the law might be fulfilled in us, who walk not according to the flesh but according to the Spirit.

—Romans 8:3–4, ESV

God's law has been fulfilled in us through Christ, His law is written on our hearts, and all this is accomplished by His Spirit within us. As we learn to live by the Spirit, yielding to His internal process of growth and maturity towards the nature of Christ, we fulfill the moral law of God. Being led by His Spirit is a defining quality of the children of God.

For all who are led by the Spirit of God are sons of God. *For you did not receive the spirit of slavery to fall back into fear, but you have received the Spirit of adoption as sons, by whom we cry, "Abba! Father!"*

—Romans 8:14–15, ESV (emphasis added)

As royal children we still have a responsibility to "put to death" sin (v.13), but the fulfillment of that responsibility is made possible by the power God has placed within us. Christ dismantled the power of sin for us, and now we must enforce His victory through life yielded to His Spirit.

One final thought here. It has been said sin separates us from God. Although it is true that sin allowed to stay in our lives can hinder our communion with Father God (1 Peter 3:7, Isaiah 59:2), hinder worship (Matthew 5:23–24), and hinder forgiveness (Matthew 6:15), it's important to recognize it will never hinder or separate us from His love for us. When we think of separation, we often picture something or someone moving or pulling away or hiding from something else. Sin does not cause God to withdraw His love from us. If it did, He never would have launched His plan to save a world full of sin. That whole effort was initiated and has been sustained by His love (John 3:16). Nothing can or ever will separate us from His love. Choosing to yield to His Spirit and turn from sin is an act of love in response to His love. Thanks be to God our Father He has made us free to do it!

> *For I am sure that neither death nor life, nor angels nor rulers, nor things present nor things to come, nor powers, nor height nor depth, nor anything else in all creation, will be able to separate us from the love of God in Christ Jesus our Lord.*
>
> —Romans 8:38–39, ESV

FREE TO SERVE

IRONICALLY, THE POSSIBILITY DOES EXIST FOR THOSE BLESSED WITH SUCH an immeasurable gift of becoming children of God to fall into a trap of entitlement—an overemphasis of one's own rights while devaluing others'. Spoiled children are never fun to be around! The mark of a child who has been spoiled is self-centeredness due to a lack of being challenged to think of the needs and desires of others above or even equal to their own.

Father God has measures in place to curb the development of a self-centered worldview in His children. One is His willingness to lovingly correct or discipline His children with the hope of bringing us back into alignment with who we really are (Hebrews 12:6). A second method is a little more indirect but no less effective. In John 13, Jesus decides to give His disciples another important object lesson concerning a defining principle of His Kingdom. Jesus gathers His disciples around Him and performs a startling gesture designed to offend the religious mindsets in the room (something He did often during His time on earth) to cause them to make a choice. Would they receive His teaching or remain wrapped up in their own way of thinking?

[Jesus] rose from supper. He laid aside his outer garments, and taking a towel, tied it around his waist. Then he poured water into a basin and began to wash the disciples' feet and to wipe them with the towel that was wrapped around him. He came to Simon Peter, who said to him, "Lord, do you wash my feet?" Jesus answered him, "What I am doing you do not understand now, but afterward you will understand." Peter said to him, "You shall never wash my feet." Jesus answered him, "If I do not wash you, you have no share with me." Simon Peter said to him, "Lord, not my feet only but also my hands and my head!"

—John 13:4–9, ESV

Although there are different speculations on what the washing of feet signified in a literal sense, the greater teaching here is a message on serving and having a servant's heart towards one another. Jesus clarifies this in verses 12–15:

*When He had washed their feet and put on His outer garments and resumed His place, he said to them, "Do you understand what I have done to you? You call me Teacher and Lord, and you are right, for so I am. If I then, your Lord and Teacher, have washed your feet, **you also ought to wash one another's feet**. For I have given you an example, that you also should do just as I have done to you."* (ESV, emphasis added)

Although our culture no longer follows the custom of washing feet, the principles Jesus was relaying still remain a source of revelation for us. Washing of the feet of family and guests of the family in a wealthy home was a job performed by the servants. It was considered a lowly position (I Samuel 25:41) and one that signified humility (I Timothy 5:10). Jesus, Himself the Son of God, was teaching those who were about to become sons of God through His death a principle on serving one another. Perhaps prompted by the disciples' previous immature fighting as to who would be the greatest in the kingdom (Luke 9:46–48), Jesus reveals a necessary humility to be found within the hearts of the children of God, hearts not opposed to serving. Many places in scripture exhort us to live a life of service both to God and to mankind.

> *I appeal to you therefore, brothers, by the mercies of God, to present your bodies as a living sacrifice, holy and acceptable to God, which is your spiritual worship.*
>
> —Romans 12:1, ESV

> *For you were called to freedom, brothers. Only do not use your freedom as an opportunity for the flesh, but* **through love serve one another**.
>
> —Galatians 5:13, ESV (emphasis added)

The task is not only to come to a place where we see and value ourselves as children of God, but to recognize that same value is also placed on our brothers and sisters around us! Does this mean we do not have to serve anyone who does not yet share our relationship with Christ? Paul didn't think so: *"For though I am free from all, I have made myself a servant to all, that I might win more of them"* (I Corinthians 9:19).

With Jesus as our example, the heart of service must become what marks us as children of God. *"The son of Man came not to be served but to serve"* (Matthew 20:28, ESV).

The revelation of who we are remains incomplete if we understand ourselves only within one identity to the exclusion of the other. **We are both servants and sons—or rather, sons who serve.** If you know yourself only to be a servant of God, you will never lay claim to your inheritance as a son. If you know yourself only to be a son, without recognizing the need to serve, you will never receive the rewards of being a faithful servant and displaying the heart of the Kingdom.

Within us must co-exist both the confidence of sons and the humility of servants. Service is a heart reaction to the love of God. We did not earn our position, therefore we do not risk losing it by bending to serve someone else. Jesus was the exact representation of God (Hebrews 1:3) and as such washed the disciples' feet. The most powerful being humbled Himself to serve mankind. Think about it. Such humility should arrest our hearts as we seek to interact with others daily. Jesus never flaunted His position as the Son of God (not to mention the King of Kings and Lord of Lords!) to rightly avoid a duty to serve. In fact, He *came* to serve and His

> Within us must co-exist both the confidence of sons and the humility of servants.

whole life and death was marked by that service. We must let Him continue to be our example today as children of God when we are presented with the opportunity to view our brothers and sisters through the honor they deserve and choose to serve them.

Let us confront attitudes of pride and self-centeredness which are not representative of who we are! And let us instead take on the attitude of servants from the security as children of God. Let us offer ourselves with the hope that those we serve will encounter the One inside of us who will meet all their needs. Let's give Him the opportunity to touch them through our lives as we extend the grace we've found ourselves enrobed in as dearly loved and blessed children.

SATISFACTION

God the Father has unloaded immense blessings upon every person who returns to Him and accepts His offer to receive it all as children through salvation. His goodness is overwhelming and He's made it clear in scripture that it is His desire to bless us: *"'For I know the plans I have for you,' declares the Lord, 'plans to prosper you and not to harm you to give you hope and a future'"* (Jeremiah 29:11, NIV, emphasis added).

Having received all His goodness, though, a child of God can fall into a state which moves beyond godly contentment and into a counterfeit called satisfaction. There is a state in which you can exclaim, "He (God) satisfies my soul" (Psalm 107:9) at the revelation that He satisfies all your needs and even the deepest longings of our souls! This is great and not the type of satisfaction I'm referring to in this section.

The Israelites were famous for falling into the type of satisfaction we're going to look at here. The book of Hosea is a tragic yet beautiful portrayal of the love of the Father in the face of His people's betrayal. You can hear many times throughout this book the cry of His heart for His children. In the middle of Hosea is a warning not only for the featured characters but for all who would be called God's people for all time. After lamenting Israel's decisions to serve other gods and give themselves over to various evil practices, God the Father explains the devastating condition which led His people to their destruction:

> *But I have been the Lord your God ever since you came out of Egypt. You shall acknowledge no God but me, no Savior except me. I cared for you in the wilderness, in the land of burning heat.*
>
> *When I fed them, they were satisfied;* **when they were satisfied, they became proud; then they forgot me**.
>
> —Hosea 13:4–6, NIV

Somewhere along the way, happily dependent Israel became satisfied. That satisfaction led to pride, and in their pride they forgot about God. It was a sequence and it's a progression we can find creeping into our lives today as children of God. Once the need is taken away, the pursuit of the Father also vanishes. Israelites were notorious for seeking God in times of need and consistently leaving Him in times of fulfillment. Although we can feel the pull towards this in our own lives, it is not how it has to be. God intends to bless His children without incurring this final result. The state of being too satisfied was not the direct result of blessing, but it's what happened to the hearts of Israel in blessing that became the gateway to the path of destruction they chose.

Living in a nation like Canada is certainly a blessing. Just the other day I was astounded by how many versions of the Bible in print I own, not to mention the versions available on my phone catapulting the access to resources to an incredible figure! With grocery stores on every corner and the majority of us reasonably employed, it can be easy to lose the sense of need that will otherwise drive us to look for a Provider. This can happen on a spiritual level as well as the physical. If we look closer at Israel's predicament in Hosea 13, we can see the real precursor to their sinful state was not being satisfied with blessing, but the heart attitude that came as a result of no longer feeling the lack within them. Pride—an ugly antagonist that's plagued mankind since the garden and caused even angels to forfeit God's blessing (Isaiah14:12–14, Ezekiel 28:12–18). The Amplified Bible gives us a definition of pride which ties in well with the depiction of it in the Israelites.

> *For all that is in the world—the lust and sensual craving of the flesh and the lust and longing of the eyes and the boastful pride of life [pretentious confidence in one's resources or in the stability of earthly things]—these do not come from the Father, but are from the world.*
> —I John 2:16, AMP

Pride is assurance in one's *own* resources. To be assured you have sufficiently sourced yourself, you will need to have forgotten the One from which it all came. That's exactly what happened to Israel when they forgot that what satisfied them had come from God. Israel had become completely satisfied and, in this case, when their stomachs were full, they no longer felt in need. Think for a moment about what typically happens at a gathering around a big meal like Christmas. Christmas is an occasion in which most of us stretch the limits on what our stomachs and digestive systems were ever intended to handle just to get in one last bite of our favorite pie! Then, once we finally throw in the flag of surrender and admit we've had enough, we exclaim, "I'm too full! I couldn't possibly have anymore!" Once our stomachs are too full, we simply cannot fit in anymore! In fact, we lose the hunger for more and no longer sense a need for more. We need our stomachs to become empty again in order to feel the need for food return. **Emptiness creates hunger.**

> Emptiness creates hunger.

This physical reality correlates closely to a spiritual one. If and when we become too full of ourselves, we lose the sense of need for our Heavenly Father and for others. We forget that none of us, in reality, is completely self-made. We were all *made*. The abilities, gifts, and talents we have to create wealth and do things for ourselves all came to us by design of the Master Creator. The position of sonship through salvation is a gift we receive and do not earn! In the same way that a heart of service comes from an elevation of value for God and others, humility towards our Father comes from a recognition of who He is and what He has done. As we empty ourselves of pride, we will feel the need for Him return and our passion for Him ignite.

Jesus' attitude as He journeyed to the cross should continually challenge us to empty ourselves of pride and make room in our hearts for the Father.

Have this mind among yourselves, which is yours in Christ Jesus, who, though He was in the form of God, did not count equality with God a thing to be grasped, **but emptied himself,** *by taking the form of a servant, being born in the likeness of men.*

—Philippians 2:5–7, ESV (emphasis added)

Unfortunately, it often took a humbling event for Israel to begin to feel the need for God again. So is the answer to be kept in a state of poverty or without blessing? Many saints throughout church history seemed to believe this was the answer. But God displays His desire to bless His children throughout the Bible and promises prosperity to us despite our tendency toward forgetfulness. He shows no fear of our potential failure when He promises to meet all our needs and even provide excess to us (2 Corinthian 9:11, Philippians 4:19)!

It is true that a state of great blessing potentially *could* lead to pride and an unhealthy satisfaction, but it certainly does not have to! If we watch over the attitude of our hearts, we can learn how to live fully satisfied by the goodness of our Father and not lose the humility and love towards Him we ought to have. The external circumstance does not have to determine our inward condition. We can learn to sail successfully aboard the lavished vessel of sonship and we can live well and walk humbly before our God and Father even in the midst of great success and financial contentment. It's a matter of the heart! It's about remembering what He's done and who He is so that thankfulness remains foremost in our minds and produces the desire to have more of Him. In this way, we will stay hungry and aware of His involvement in our lives. In this freedom you can carry on into all the blessings the Father has made available to you!

He escorts me to the banquet hall; it's obvious how much He loves me.
—Song of Solomon 2:4, NLT

A LABOUR OF LOVE

. . .but Jesus went to the Mount of Olives. Early in the morning he came again to the temple. All the people came to him, and he sat down and taught them. The scribes and the Pharisees brought a woman who had been caught in adultery, and placing her in the midst they said to him, "Teacher, this woman has been caught in the act of adultery. Now in the Law, Moses commanded us to stone such women. So what do you say?" This they said to test him, that they might have some charge to bring against him. Jesus bent down and wrote with his finger on the ground. And as they continued to ask him, he stood up and said to them, "Let him who is without sin among you be the first to throw a stone at her." And once more he bent down and wrote on the ground. But when they heard it, they went away one by one, beginning with the older ones, and Jesus was left alone with the woman standing before him. Jesus stood up and said to her, "Woman, where are they? Has no one condemned you?" She said, "No one, Lord." And Jesus said, "Neither do I condemn you; go, and from now on sin no more."

—John 8:1–11, ESV

THIS CHAPTER IN JOHN OPENS WITH ONE OF THE MOST STUNNING stories depicting the heart of grace the Kingdom of God operates from. The Pharisees and Scribes accusingly drove a woman caught in adultery into the centre of the crowd while they remained a safe distance from her and her sin. Jesus, in the face of overt human failure, chose a dramatically different approach than they expected. He knelt down, refusing to remain "above" her even in His sinless perfection.

His humility begins to condemn the crowd and eventually they are forced to drop *their* charges against her due to the impossible qualification Jesus sets up as a right to judge others—without sin. This standard, however, was one Jesus had achieved and once it was only the two of them left, with every right to condemn her He, instead, chooses not to! He simply leaves her with a command to go and sin no more.

In this gracious act, Jesus, carrying the heart of the Father, demonstrates He's after something deeper. His refusal to stand at a distance from the woman revealed a willingness to come alongside her and help her get free. What He did for this woman foreshadowed what He would eventually do for the whole world on the cross—offer Himself to bring freedom to all who would receive and reconnect the children of God to the Father. While the Pharisees demanded strict adherence to the law and condemnation of all who did not follow it, Jesus attempted to connect with the erring woman as if to try to win her heart. He first showed mercy before He requested her to leave her sin. He wanted the basis for her new life of righteousness to be His love and grace demonstrated through mercy.

While religious teaching is after outward behavior modification, heaven's perspective focuses much more on the heart. Jesus later equated obedience to an act of love: *"If you love me, you will keep my commandments"* (John 14:15, ESV). John echoes this in his message in 1 John 5:8: *"For this is the love of God that we keep His commandments"* (ESV). Jesus' approach to sin demonstrates a desire of the Father to have His children living from their hearts loving Him in all they do as a response to His love.

As previously stated, sin is a destructive force seeking to separate us from our Father, the source of all we need. Sin entangles and weighs us down! (Hebrews 12:1, NIV)

Sin comes in all its various forms in order to separate us, bind us up, and get us to believe lies so we're hindered in our run. When we partner with it and allow it to become a part of us, it always brings destruction, which the Father is desperately trying to avoid.

> *But each person is tempted when he is lured and enticed by his own desire. Then desire when it has conceived gives birth to sin, and sin when it is fully grown brings forth death.*
>
> —James 1:14–15, ESV

Receiving Father's command to "sin no more" with an understanding of His love and the destructiveness of sin can help us come to appreciate what He's trying to do in our lives. When we connect with His heart *for* us, our hearts engage and it becomes easy to want to let ourselves be *for* Him. Furthermore, He did not give us such a command without providing for us the power we would need to fulfill it in our lives!

He has set us up for victory through the cross! He does not demand we adhere to a list of impossible regulations while He stands at a distance. The Father offered His son, the Son offered His life, and His Spirit offers His power to break free from all sin that tries to hinder us. He is incredibly involved in our freedom and this all stems from His heart of love for us. God is love and love is what His kingdom runs on!

He desires His children of the Kingdom to operate from love as well. When Jesus was asked to relay what the most important commandment was, I mean the one we really need to know and follow, His answer was this: *"love the Lord your God with all your heart, all your soul, and all your mind"* (Matthew 22:37, NLT, emphasis added). He essentially boiled down all the requirements of the kingdom to one central motivation—love your God. Sometimes as Christians we can miss the heart of God by thinking our behavior is what matters most. He made it clear, however, that He does not like good or even great behavior without the heart involved!

> *These people honor me with their lips, but their hearts are far from me.*
> —Matthew 15:8, NLT

> *I desire steadfast love and not sacrifice, the knowledge of God rather than burnt offerings.*
>
> —Hosea 6:6, ESV

In the same way that the Father's main motivation for seeking out relationship with us is love (John 3:16), He desires love be the motivation behind our seeking and serving Him. We can serve anyone, but until love is involved there will be some level of distance between us and the one we're serving.

My husband, a talented carpenter and handyman, often pulls out an epoxy glue to fix various things in need of repair. Epoxy is a very strong two-part adhesive that, when combined, seals two objects together. Like epoxy, two components need to exist within the heart of a Christian to enable them to fulfill the highest law of love Christ set out for us. These are love and thankfulness. Love and thankfulness combined form a powerful bonding agent in the human heart. That agent is devotion. Devotion is the glue that will hold us closer to the Father than any law could ever do.

When you hear an account of someone who has been pulled from a burning building or some other life-threatening event, you'll often find they responded, "I don't know how I could ever thank them! I'd do anything for them." Picture what it would be like to be in a situation where you were sure you were going to die, there was no way out, and all hope was lost. You've even started preparing for it emotionally and mentally and then all of sudden someone makes it to you. Someone risked their life to pull you out and give you back yours! How would you feel towards them?

Well, in reality that *is* what Christ did for us, commissioned by the Father to come get you. We were dead without hope and He gave His life to make us alive and give us all hope of eternal life! A lot of us will experience deep gratitude towards the Father for our salvation, but without a proper view of the Father's heart towards us and our worth and value to Him as children, the love part can be replaced by fear as we become increasingly aware of the debt we owe Him. Love and fear cannot coexist. One always casts out the other (I John 4:18). That's why we need to be continually perfected in His love. As we are, all Christian conduct begins to be a labour of love instead of a service of fear. In this way all we do *for* Him—tithing, attending church, teaching, preaching, worshipping—becomes an outflow of the love and relationship we share with our Father.

There are many attitudes and behaviours clearly laid out in scripture as sinful and displeasing to the Father, but the compliance God seeks is to come from the heart. It doesn't mean we shouldn't obey if we don't feel like it or feel love in it. Obedience out of love is the end goal of our Christian lives. So as we're growing, there may be decisions that feel like obedience only, but even those are an act of love.

The goal is to get so close to Him our heart wonders why it would ever leave Him. To be so enamoured with Him the things of the world lose their appeal. Love is the goal. We receive His love and then respond with all our love to Him. We will find any chains of bondage to sin breaking easily as we become devoted sons and daughters of God, because we know His heart and receive so much from Him already. We will be glad to say, "Have your way, Father; here's all I am because you give all you are to me."

Rules may produce good behaviour, but they cannot produce devotion. That's why the Father's plan to bring us back to Himself is one of grace and mercy. Grace and mercy when understood and received by the human heart produce devotion, and devotion is what the Father really wants.

For in Christ Jesus neither circumcision nor uncircumcision counts for anything, but only faith working through love.

—Galatians 5:6, ESV

PART IV

THE ULTIMATE
SERVANT SON

DEVELOPING ROYAL DISPOSITIONS

The Son of man came not to be served but to serve, and to give his life as a ransom for many.

—Mark 10:45, ESV

Although he was a son, he learned obedience through what he suffered.
—Hebrews 5:8, ESV

WE'RE GOING TO CONCLUDE THIS BOOK FOCUSING ON OUR GREATEST example of true sonship—Jesus. As the archetype of sonship and servanthood, He left us a beautiful portrayal of what our lives ultimately can be in the presence of God the Father. In Philippians 2 we are instructed to pattern our lives after Jesus, particularly in the area of attitude.

Your attitude should be the same as that of Christ Jesus: *Who, being in very nature God, did not consider equality with God something to be grasped, but made Himself nothing taking the very nature of servant.*

—Philippians 2:5–7, NIV (emphasis added)

Attitude determines a lot in life. Many high-achieving athletes and professionals attribute their success in life to attitude. I have often heard the saying, "Attitude determines altitude!" It is true that keeping a healthy attitude can bring us through a lot and help us to achieve more than we thought possible.

This passage, however, asks us to consider the attitude of someone much greater than even the most superlative human hero this world has ever produced. Attitude is more than just a feeling or posture towards something. In its definition it carries with it the meaning of a "disposition, manner, tendency, or orientation" towards something. An attitude, in a sense, is a "way of being."

In this section we're going to cover eight attitudes Christ displayed that, when found present within us, contribute profoundly to our ability to live well as sons and daughters of God. My heart is thrilled to end here with what I hope will be a revelatory look at the One who deserves all the glory and all the honor, Jesus Christ. My hope is that you are enamoured with Him and awed by His beauty as the One who purchased our pathway home to this wonderful privilege we have as children of God. We owe it all to Him, so let Him be glorified!

ATTITUDE OF HUMILITY

Being found in appearance as a man **He humbled Himself** *and became obedient to death.*

—Philippians 2:8, NIV

There are so many places in the gospels where the humility of Christ shines through. In fact, His very act of leaving His place in heaven to come and serve sinful humanity is the characterization of humility itself. This Son, Jesus, is the One through whom God, *"Made the universe"* (Hebrews 1:2). He is *"the radiance of God's glory and the exact representation of His being, sustaining all things by His powerful word"* (Hebrews 1:3, NIV). He is the King of Kings and Lord of Lords and a full-fledged member of the Trinity. He is God. Yet, He did not *"consider equality with God something to be grasped..."* (Philippians 2:6) as He willingly gave His life to live and die among us *for* us.

This attitude of Christ is in stark contrast to someone else whose goal was to be like God and even overtake Him—Satan. Satan exuded an attitude of pride which is the antithesis of humility (see Ezekiel 28:12–19, Isaiah 14:12–14). While Satan was bent on building his own empire, hungry for power and complete control, Jesus securely and temporarily laid aside all He had in order to come to us.

In his book, Humility: The Beauty of Holiness, Andrew Murray makes this statement about humility: "Jesus came to bring humility back to earth, to make us partakers of it and by it to save us...His humility is our salvation. His salvation is our humility."[13] I think it's an astounding statement that Jesus came to bring humility back to earth. You see, humility is a heavenly quality. And it is one God the Father exhibits on a continual basis marked by His relentless pursuit of love towards a world that rejects Him. Humility is the quality that allows an all-powerful, all-knowing being to give

---

13 Murray, Andrew. *Humility: The Beauty of Holiness.*

Himself so freely for us. Deep down, the roots of pride are often embedded in fear. Because God is completely secure and there is no fear in Him for He is love and love casts out fear, He was able to take the attitude of a servant to mankind embodied in Christ.

When we become secure in who we are as children of God, we will not fear laying down our own desires if needed to serve the Father and others. When we know our destinies are secure and our needs will be met, we can live beyond ourselves. We can surrender the quest for our own wisdom in favour of receiving the superior wisdom of God through His word and Spirit! We can trust His still, small voice of direction for our lives knowing it will be much better than even the greatest plan we could conceive!

The example of humility Father God sets up through Christ ought to bring us to the end of ourselves. It is truly amazing! As we adopt this attitude for ourselves, we will see its great fruit in our lives. All the good things pride attempts to steal from us will be ours. Jesus was willing to do it all because He saw "the joy set before Him." He saw the bigger picture, which was the potential salvation of the world and so much more. Humility gives us the ability to see past ourselves and live lives which affect and enrich the world around us.

ATTITUDE OF AUTHORITY

I find encouragement in the fact that Jesus had a human, natural side to Him and that it was the lens through which the natural world saw Him. He was a carpenter's son whose family was shrouded with mystery and even possible scandal from His birth. He had brothers and sisters and grew up like any other child does in this world.

As Jesus grew up, however, you can start to see a clash between His human side and identity as God incarnate with a Heavenly mandate to save the world. One day, Jesus' earthly family tries to get Him to "do the right thing" in their eyes when they come to visit Him (Mark 3:21, 31–35). But Jesus takes this opportunity to continue defining who He really is and turns the situation into a lesson about His true family.

Many times we forget that we're looking back at Jesus through the pages of the Bible and His completed work on the cross and resurrection. It's important to note, though, everyone around Him saw Him from the natural side. One time the people's inability to get past the natural hindered them from seeing the supernatural in their town (Mark 6:1–6). Although it would likely have been confusing for the people around Him at first, Jesus didn't shy away from making a distinction about who He *really* was. Jesus unapologetically admitted He was the Son of God (Luke 22:70, Matthew 16:15–17) and let that identity be the truth from which He lived. As such, He knew He had authority and used it to *"destroy the works of the devil"* which was part of His life's work on the earth, and continues on today (1 John 3:8, ESV).

Though Jesus did display an incredible attitude of humility, He also walked secure in His authority. As previously discussed in this book, we too, as children of God, walk in authority because we are in Christ. Therefore, we have the opportunity to walk securely like Jesus did. True security comes from knowing who we are and what we are made for. When we're secure, we don't need to compensate with things like arrogance or pride. We can simply walk in authority.

Jesus knew He was loved by the Father (John 17:23); Jesus knew where His authority came from and He knew what He was made for. As the revelation of sonship continues to grow in us, we can walk in greater levels of authority, tolerating less and less the lies of the enemy in our daily lives. Jesus was not frail or a wimp when He walked the earth; He didn't need to be. He knew who He was and asserted that throughout His life.

ATTITUDE OF COURAGE

Courage…what a desirous quality! Wouldn't we all love to be deemed as courageous people, especially when it comes to areas of faith, family, and the future? There is nothing more symbolic of courage and bravery than a soldier depicted as fit, stone-faced, and ready for battle in the name of freedom. There is no doubt a soldier needs courage in huge doses in the horrific circumstances of war.

But Christianity is also depicted as a feat which requires significant courage. Jesus often exhorted His followers to have courage—for example, when He asked them, *"Have you still no faith?"* (Mark 4:40, ESV). But that's faith, you say, not courage. Well, let's see if I can convince you of the connection between the two.

What is courage? Courage is "the quality of mind or spirit that enables a person to face difficulty, danger, pain, etc. without fear; bravery."[14] Coupled with synonyms like fearlessness, adventurousness, backbone, determination, fortitude, heroism, nerve, tenac-

---

14 "Courage" Dictionary.com (accessed May 13, 2017)

ity, and valor, courage is certainly a word I would love to have in a description of me.

Does courage, though, exist in some individuals and not in others? Where does it come from? Jesus implies a remarkable clue in Mark 4:40 how courage can be attained. He asks the disciples a startling question in the midst of their distress about the storm they're facing: *"Why are you still so afraid? Have you still no faith?"* (ESV) These questions imply that if the disciples had faith they would not have fear. If they did not have fear, the storm would not have been a big deal to them. And if the storm was not threatening to them, they would have faced it *bravely.* If we saw them fearlessly riding the waves, Peter at the bow screaming at the top of his lungs, "Woohoo, what a ride!" it could have been said they were showing great tenacity, nerve, fortitude, determination, and even adventurousness. In the next breath, we could ascribe courage to their actions, all made possible by faith.

See, faith creates courage in us. If courage was just some rare characteristic of a fortunate few, it wouldn't be fair for both God the Father and Jesus to demand it of us so many places in the Bible, just like the story of the Fig Tree found in Mark. At first glance, it may appear Jesus is a bit unreasonable as He curses a fig tree for not having fruit for Him (after all, we all get a bit spastic when we're hungry and this was a particularly bad day for Him), but verses 20–24 reveal a possible motive for Jesus' behaviour: to teach the disciples something.

> *As they passed by in the morning, they saw the fig tree withered away to its roots. And Peter remembered and said to him, "Rabbi, look! The*

fig tree that you cursed has withered." And Jesus answered them, "Have faith in God. Truly, I say to you, whoever says to this mountain, 'Be taken up and thrown into the sea,' and does not doubt in his heart, but believes that what he says will come to pass, it will be done for him. Therefore I tell you, whatever you ask in prayer, believe that you have received it, and it will be yours.

—Mark 11:20–24, ESV

Jesus takes the opportunity to teach His followers about faith. And He elaborates by encouraging them that if they have faith they will also have the courage to believe and ask for anything and see it happen! See, courage is the will to act which faith provides.

Jesus displayed courage on a regular basis. Well, you say, He was God so that doesn't count. If we look at Acts 10:38, we are confronted with how Jesus did what He did. *"How God anointed Jesus of Nazareth...for God was with Him..."* (ESV).

Jesus made this statement concerning us: *"Whoever believes in me will also do the works that I do; and greater works than these will he do, because I am going to the Father"* (John 14:12, ESV).

Jesus did what He did because God was with Him, and if we believe, we can do what He did and even more! One final encouragement from God's word: *"Do not be frightened, and do not be dismayed, for the LORD your God is with you wherever you go"* (Joshua 1:9, ESV).

God does not expect an act of courage from His people without promising to be there to make it happen. Several times in scripture He gives only one reason why His people should trust Him and courageously move ahead in faith to do what He's asking: "I am with you."

That's it! And like Jesus implied in the boat to His disciples, that truth should be all we need. I'm here, I'm in charge, now go. Be strong, be courageous, be fearless. Have faith like I have and act like I act on the earth. Like Jesus, we can stand against the impossible and work with Him to see His kingdom come on earth, for *"everything is possible for one who believes"* (Mark 9:23, NIV).

Take up faith in your heart until it produces courage within you, which will lead you to actions that will do nothing less than transform the world around you!

ATTITUDE OF HONOUR

There's an incredible story about a seemingly unnecessary miracle Jesus performed. This miracle not only served as a lesson in sonship for Peter, but also a representation of the heart of honor Jesus possessed towards His Father and mankind.

> *When they came to Capernaum, the collectors of the two-drachma tax went up to Peter and said, "Does your teacher not pay the tax?" He said, "Yes." And when he came into the house, Jesus spoke to him first, saying, "What do you think, Simon? From whom do kings of the earth take toll or tax? From their sons or from others?" And when he said, "From others," Jesus said to him, "Then the sons are free. However, not to give offense to them, go to the sea and cast a hook and take the first fish that comes up, and when you open its mouth you will find a shekel. Take that and give it to them for me and for yourself."*
>
> —Matthew 17:24–26, ESV

Not only does this story evoke in me a sense of wonder at the way Jesus decides to provide the tax for Himself and Peter, but also at Jesus' decision to pay the taxes at all so as not to "offend" man. Think about it: the Creator of the universe *paid taxes to man*. He subjected Himself to the rule of His own creation. The life of Christ in many ways depicts a supreme being honoring lesser, undeserving beings. Honor means to treat with "high respect, as for worth, merit or rank."[15] God demonstrated the worth and value He has for mankind when He sent His Son Jesus Christ to give His life for us as a sacrifice, and Jesus affirmed this honor, worth, and merit by being willing to die. When the full deity of Christ is the lens through which we observe the life of Christ, honor can be found permeating every area. One of many depictions of the honor Christ held, not only for His Father but also everything that belonged to His Father when Jesus decides to go to the Temple and ends up doing a little cleaning:

> *The Passover of the Jews was at hand, and Jesus went up to Jerusalem. In the temple he found those who were selling oxen and sheep and pigeons, and the money-changers sitting there. And making a whip of cords, he drove them all out of the temple, with the sheep and oxen. And he poured out the coins of the money-changers and overturned their tables. And he told those who sold the pigeons, "Take these things away; do not make my Father's house a house of trade." His disciples remembered that it was written, "Zeal for your house will consume me."*
>
> —John 2:13–17, ESV

---

15 "Honor" Dictionary.com (accessed May 13, 2017)

The money changers and opportunistic entrepreneurs were set up selling the expensive wares the Jews needed for the sacrifices they were required to make under the old system of law. The problem with this, besides the fact that they often charged exorbitant amounts and treated the people unfairly, is that they were set up in the Outer Court, which was the one place Gentiles were allowed to go and pray. They were not only taking advantage of the Gentiles financially but they were making the place dedicated to prayer and communion with God unusable.

This made Jesus so upset He made a whip and drove out all the money changers and merchants. The only explanation given for this display is Jesus quoting Psalm 69:9, *"Zeal for your house will consume me"* (ESV). Other accounts show Jesus clarifying His actions by stating, *"Is it not written, 'My house will be called a house of prayer for all nations?' But you have made it 'a den of robbers'"* (Mark 11:17, ESV). Jesus held His Father's house in great honor because He held His Father in great honor. The desires of His Father mattered to Him and He loved what His Father loved. Additionally, His passionate disdain of the exploitation and exclusion of the Gentiles from the temple courts reveals yet again an honor and respect Jesus had for mankind.

As stated earlier, God's very willingness to come and live among us, to submit to us and to death on a cross, was an incredible show of honor to us. **Salvation itself, sonship, *is* an honor.**

> *For the LORD takes pleasure in His people; He adorns the humble with salvation.*

> —Psalm 149:4, ESV

As we live freely in this honor of being children of God, our lives should be characterized by honour of our Father and honour of others. This doesn't mean we need to make whips and drive out the youth group's bake sale in the foyer at church (context is everything, people), but as we listen to the Holy Spirit, He will show us ways in which honor may be lacking from our lives. Honoring God the Father is to treat Him with respect, valuing Him and the things He values. There are many ways we honor the Father such as worshipping Him, bringing Him our finances, working well, surrendering to His will, etc., all of which when done from the right place show a high value for Him in us. We can respond with honour towards Him out of the honour He has given us as His sons and daughters.

> *Honor the Lord for the glory of his name. Worship the Lord in the splendor of his holiness.*
>
> —Psalm 29:2, NLT

> *Love each other with genuine affection, and take delight in honoring each other.*
>
> —Romans 12:10, NLT

ATTITUDE OF JUSTICE

A Messianic prophecy spoken about Jesus in Jeremiah 23:5–6 and repeated in Jeremiah 33:15–16 describes the next disposition of Jesus we're going to focus on—justice.

In those days and at that time I will cause a righteous Branch to spring up for David, and he shall execute justice and righteousness in the land. In those days Judah will be saved, and Jerusalem will dwell securely. And this is the name by which it will be called: "The Lord is our righteousness."

—Jeremiah 33:15–16, ESV

These passages describe Jesus as one who would do what was "just and right." Jesus lived a perfect and sinless life. He was wholly righteous, which means He did all that was truly "right" according to the standards of holiness found in the Father. Because of His "right-ness", or righteousness, He could offer to us His righteousness, and through salvation justify us, fulfilling the demands of justice. Not only did Jesus ultimately fulfill the demands of justice for mankind engrossed in sin, but He also stood for what was just and right within his society.

Jesus was often in trouble with the religious and political influences of His day, simply because His idea of what was right and good often differed drastically from theirs. Whether it was placing honor and dignity on those rejected from society by talking with them, inviting them into His ministry, healing them, or offering them the same rights as everyone else in salvation, Jesus displayed a passionate desire to see true justice come to the world around Him.

We live in a world where pain and injustice are all around us. Just half an hour watching the news can bring enough discouragement to cause us to try to find a safe place out of all the craziness in the world. But the Bible implores people of God to bring justice, peace, and mercy to the world around us. The Bible is littered with references asking us to remember the poor, stand up for the weak, clothe and feed those in need, and perform many other acts of love to affect change in the world around (Psalm 82:3; Psalm 112:9; Proverbs 14:31, Proverbs 19:17; 2 Corinthians 9; James 1:27).

In Isaiah 58:6–8, God reveals His heart's desire to have His people live a lifestyle that cares about the world around them and carry His kingdom to the lives around them. He delivers a convincing speech exposing the superficiality in the way they were fulfilling religious duties (fasting) while treating others unfairly and fighting with one another.

> *Is not this the fast that I choose: to loose the bonds of wickedness, to undo the straps of the yoke, to let the oppressed to go free, and to break every yoke? Is it not to share your bread with the hungry and bring the homeless poor into your house; when you see the naked, to cover him, and not to hide yourself from your own flesh? Then shall your light break forth like the dawn, and your healing shall spring up speedily; your righteousness shall go before you; the glory of the Lord shall be your rear guard.*
>
> —Isaiah 58:6–8, ESV

In this passage, God is commanding His people not only to help the poor and care about injustice, but to be the people who eradicate it. For most of us living in Canada, the question is not so much can we make a difference, but rather, will we? With technology advancement and increases in the average income, we have more opportunity than any previous generation to make a difference. We cannot be pacified by the demonically influenced societies we live in which tell us there is no hope. There is Hope—we know Him—His name is Jesus! As the children of God, we must begin to care about what He cares about. Letting His perspectives and passions infiltrate every area of our lives will cause us to live differently, intentionally and powerfully. We must reject apathy. We are the church of God filled with His power and positioned to overcome all things. We carry true justice, true mercy, true love, true righteousness, and these things need to be distributed all over our places of influence. **Every time we move with the passion of Father God, we will move with His power** and His power is still unlimited, unchanging, and unstoppable. Decide to be a vessel for His use in your neighborhood, workplace, school, family, etc., because as God's people we are meant to be world changers in many ways.

Stand up and speak out under the direction of the Holy Spirit! Love radically and care deeply. In doing this, we embody the values of Christ and we will see His kingdom come on earth as it is in heaven.

ATTITUDE OF COMPASSION

We cannot look at the life of Jesus and miss perhaps the most discernible characteristic of all. It's love. Jesus lived a life of love perfectly emulating the character of Father God, who is love, since He was the *"exact representation"* of Him (Hebrews 1:3, NIV). Jesus as our earthly example walked out this love in one particularly challenging way.

Once Jesus' ministry officially began, things got crazy. He tried to keep a lid on who He was and what He was doing early on (Mark

1:44), but word got out, and as it did, Jesus had to deal with crowds and crowds of people hounding Him. It is in the moments when I read about Him ministering all day and seemingly trying to get away with his disciples only to be met by more people somewhere else, that I become challenged by how Jesus responded. He would pour out of Himself, the ministries of heaven, onto these people and continue to meet the needs of broken humanity. And what was it inside of Him that led to this response? Mark highlights the underlying condition of Jesus' heart that enabled Him to respond to the needy. *"When he went ashore he saw a great crowd, and he **had compassion on them**, because they were like sheep without a shepherd. And he began to teach them many things"* (Mark 6:34, ESV, emphasis added).

Jesus was moved by compassion. He didn't act kindly towards mankind out of obligated duty or because His dad made Him do it. He acted from His heart. He was compelled by compassion, which led Him to walk about His day from a heart of love. He essentially was love—walking. He went about His day with the heart of God leading and that made Him open and available to others. **Love was Jesus' lifestyle, not just an intermittent state.**

Peter and John seemed to have caught at least a glimpse of the lifestyle of love Jesus displayed. In Acts 3, the two are on their way to go and pray when a crippled man asks them for some money and Peter responds above and beyond the man's initial request. First, he stops just like Jesus often did. Moved with compassion, Peter stops what he is intending to do that day long enough to seize the opportunity to let God do what *He* wants to do. In his usual straightforward manner, Peter acknowledges the man and with the eyes of Jesus he perceives the real need. Peter then freely gives what he has received: the power of the Holy Spirit within him, moving in healing.

Within all of us as believers and children of God is the answer to every problem we will face in the world: Jesus. The problem is we fail to recognize it. Because of this, we go about too many of our days without the intention of letting God touch the world around and through us. We can miss the chance to love-walk, which is where the heart of the Father moves the heart of the son to reach the one in need.

We need our lives as Christians to resemble this pattern of living laid out by Jesus. Though He did rest, and taught His disciples to rest, Christ responded to opportunities that came to Him to impact the world around Him. I will leave you with this encouragement from the words of Ephesians 5:1–2:

> *Follow God's example, therefore, as dearly loved children and walk in the way of love, just as Christ loved us and gave himself up for us as a fragrant offering and sacrifice to God.* (NIV)

ATTITUDE OF SELF-DENIAL

For this next attitude, we're going to take a glimpse at a scenario involving Jesus and His disciples recounted in Mark 8:31–38. Things are going well for Jesus at this point. Apart from the usual run-ins with the disgruntled religious leaders of His day, His ministry continues to grow as He is training up some fine young men and drawing large crowds whenever He speaks. The Kingdom is coming to earth through Him as He moves with power for healings and miracles, a ministry many today would love to have!

Right in the middle of His growing success, He decides to tell His followers about the way His life will end in the not so distant future and the seemingly dire purpose God had for His life—He would be rejected, then die and rise again.

Undoubtedly this was a shocker for all the disciples in some regard, but Peter, being the spokesman that he was, decided to say something about it. Scripture tells us that Peter *"took Him aside and began to rebuke Him"* (Mark 8:32, ESV). Wow, rebuke Jesus, the Son of God, Peter, really? We have to remember we have the opportunity to look back at the situation post-cross and Jesus' ascension to heaven. These men were still trying to figure out in some sense who Jesus really was and even though Peter had correctly identified Jesus as the Christ (v. 29), he had very little idea what that truly meant.

After hearing Peter's "suggestions," Jesus recognizes their true source and calls out the devil's influence on his mind (v. 33). Jesus then expounds upon this, addressing the crowd and, with His words recorded in the Bible, all who would wish to follow Him in the future.

> *And calling the crowd to him with his disciples, he said to them, "If anyone would come after me, let him deny himself and take up his cross and follow me. For whoever would save his life will lose it, but whoever loses his life for my sake and the gospel's will save it. For what does it profit a man to gain the whole world and forfeit his soul? For what can a man give in return for his soul? For whoever is ashamed of me and of my words in this adulterous and sinful generation, of*

him will the Son of Man also be ashamed when he comes in the glory of his Father with the holy angels.

—Mark 8:34–38, ESV

When I first read this scripture I felt a bit conflicted. If I apply it solely to the level of prosperity I enjoy as a result of being born and raised in an affluent country such as Canada, I can begin to feel ashamed of all the good things I have—a home, car, loads of food in my cupboards, and so on. It's almost enough to make me wonder, "Should I sell everything and move to a hut in Africa?" Well, the Bible indicates you can do that and still get it wrong (1 Corinthians 13:3). So, what exactly was Jesus saying? I would like to suggest that applying this scripture only to prosperity or monetary wealth would be to abate the point Jesus is trying to make.

Scripture is not opposed to prosperity. Observing the way God blessed His people throughout the Bible reveals a direct correlation between the abundant blessing of God manifesting in such things as wealth, health, peace, etc. and the closeness of the people's relationship with God. But here, in the main text of this section, something prompted Jesus to deliver a message essentially highlighting self-denial.

The answer may be found in the verses leading up to His message. In verses 31 and 32, Jesus informs the young men about the plan God had for His life and this plan involved temporary earthly suffering. Peter, who obviously completely missed the part about Jesus "rising again," didn't like what he heard. Why? Well, if we draw from Peter's later denials of Christ, we can gather that he, like all mankind, had some lingering fears about the rejection of men and death. This, perhaps, was all brought on by a skewed perception of what a successful life and ministry should have looked like for Jesus. Peter didn't want to die like Jesus and he didn't want to die for Him.

Though many of us, thankfully, will not be asked to die *for* Christ physically, we have all been asked to die *with* Him spiritually (Romans 6:4, 8; Galatians 2:20; Colossians 2:20). Jesus was describing to His disciples the plans and purpose God had for His life, which in the end would accomplish something far greater and have farther reaching impact than the totality of the young men's intellect could ever dream of. Therefore, they were limited to thinking about "the things of men" and not "the things of God." He then addresses a crowd whose reality in that day was almost certain persecution for following Him.

In our North American culture, we can increasingly feel society's move away from the things of God in favor of the things of men. Jesus lays out a challenge in this passage not only for those facing persecution but for us also to reject the pull to be consumed by these values. "Losing our life" for the sake of Christ in order to gain true life may look different in each believer. Whether it's a moral conviction which results in the jeers of those who call you "old fashioned" or declaring God is real and alive in spite of the fact you may be viewed as foolish and uneducated, it all matters! You may be called to sell everything or you may be called to make a ton of money in order to become the hands and feet through which God can bless the earth and proclaim His gospel.

Whatever purpose God has designed you for, the question we have to answer is, will we consider His purposes for our lives and choose to say yes? Will our heart posture be the same as Jesus' in the garden of Gethsemane—*"not my will, but yours, be done"* (Luke 22:42, ESV)?

To be alive is to have been given life, and our lives are not our own (I Corinthians 6:19–20). Let us live open-hearted and open-handed, submitted to God Our Father whose only intent toward us is good.

ATTITUDE OF FAITHFULNESS

We're going to end this section on perhaps one of the most esteemed attitude found in Christ, and that is faithfulness. Faithfulness, when observed, certainly brings respect and honour, but it can be a difficult attitude to master in tough situations.

Jesus was and is faithful. He is noted as such in Hebrews 3:2: *"He [Jesus] was faithful to the one who appointed Him"* and verse 6, *"but Christ is faithful as the Son over God's house"* (NIV). The attitude of faithfulness is perhaps most famously noted in reference to the Parable of the Talents in Matthew 25. The two "faithful" servants took what they were given—one five talents, the other two—and invested them, putting them to work to gain a good reward for their master. This in contrast to the "wicked" servant who dug a hole and buried the talent he had been given. Something different in the first two servants led them to desire to do something with what they had been given, and although their actions are highlighted in this passage, the motivation for their actions is the treasure we're digging for here.

Faithfulness is described as "strict or thorough in the performance of duty; true to one's word, promises, vows, etc.; steady in allegiance or affection; reliable, trusted or believed."[16] Wow, what a powerful word! In the Bible, "faithfulness" is described by what a person did. But what causes someone to be faithful?

Behind faithful actions lies a faithful heart. Faithfulness is a high level of commitment based on love, which produces actions that reveal the love we have for someone. For instance, probably the greatest example of this is faithfulness within the context of marriage. Faithfulness in marriage is most commonly related to sexual purity and the level of commitment you show in this area to your spouse. But faithfulness is meant to go way beyond simply trying not to flirt with someone other than your spouse or abstaining from inappropriate images. Faithfulness in a marriage is to be committed body, soul, and spirit to your spouse. Contrary to popular belief, the act of sex accomplishes a bonding of two individuals so significant it binds the two together not only in body but in soul and spirit. The *"two become one"* (I Corinthians 6:16, ESV).

Incredibly, the Bible states that in salvation we actually become one with the Lord; *"but he who is joined to the Lord becomes one spirit with him"* (I Corinthians 6:17, ESV). Salvation accomplishes the work of bringing the whole person into unity with God and subsequently every member of the Trinity as they are all also one. In the same way any person would not enjoy having their spouse act faithfully solely out of duty and not love, our faithfulness towards God should come from a deep recognition that we are one with Him. It's so much deeper

---

16 Faithfulness, http://www.dictionary.com/browse/faithfulness?s=t (accessed August 8, 2017)

than duty—it is love expressing itself through loyalty. In the same way a faithful spouse forsakes all others to keep their body for the one they love, we allow our bodies to come under the authority and power of the Holy Spirit (Galatians 5:16) to turn away from temptation that would violate our love for Him. Our lives become a gift we can give back to Him out of the gratefulness we feel towards Him for giving His life for us. He is so faithful and so committed to us!

We must recognize the call to be committed to Him. Like the healthy, vibrant marriage relationship when two people truly live faithfully to one another in every area, our faithfulness to Him will produce fullness of life in and through us. After all, you cannot be completely connected to Love and not be filled with it. You cannot be bonded to Hope and not brim with it. You cannot be joined to Peace and be in lack of it. This is the closeness Jesus enjoyed faithfully connected to His Father, and so also the relationship with our Father available through Him for us.

CONCLUSION

The identity of being a child of God is the conduit through which all the promises of God flow. Inheritance is given to children, not servants. Because of this, we have to identify ourselves as true children of God through Jesus Christ and receive the inheritance of that position. We must, like Jesus said, *"Become like little children"* (Matthew 18:2–4, ESV) to inherit the kingdom.

Many times, our mind, will and emotions rise up against this notion, causing us to try to earn from God what can only be received from Him. Inheriting God's kingdom requires the laying down of all pursuit of earning anything apart from Him. It requires a return to the dependency of childhood upon a Father who is eternally good and faithful. At the root of every argument your soul may launch against this concept, some pride or fear will resist the reality of our need of Him. But we must embrace our need. We must identify ourselves as children in order to live in the glorious freedom afforded to this position.

More than I am Christian, a term first given at Antioch (Acts 11:26) identifying early believers as followers of Christ, I am a Child of God. That is my identity. However, if we only ever know ourselves as sons and daughters of God and reject the reality that we are also His servants, we may never experience the rewards servanthood brings both in this life and eternity. It is an overflow of gratitude in our hearts to Him which causes us to serve Him and others around us.

Sonship and servanthood combine to become the foundation for a vibrant, fruitful, and power-filled Christian life. There is always more to discover about who we are as children and who He is as Father. But a life journey built upon the foundation of a restored relationship with God the Father through Christ will lead us into the depths of the Father's love for us. It will lead us into the best He desires for us in every area of life.

Bless you as you journey forward in this revelation. Father intends your life to be the grandest adventure!